JACK HYLTON
PRESENTS

Pamela W. Logan

BFI PUBLISHING

First published in 1995 by the
British Film Institute
21 Stephen Street
London W1P 2LN

The British Film Institute exists to promote appreciation, enjoyment,
protection and development of moving image culture in and throughout the
whole of the United Kingdom. Its activities include the National Film and
Television Archive; the National Film Theatre; the Museum of the Moving
Image; the London Film Festival; the production and distribution of film
and video; funding and support for regional activities; Library and
Information Services; Stills, Posters and Designs; Research; Publishing
and Education; and the monthly *Sight and Sound* magazine.

British Library Cataloguing in Publication Data.
A catalogue record for this book is available from the
British Library.

ISBN: 0–85170–551–0

Cover by Push
Front cover still: June Whitfield and Tony Hancock
                    in *The Tony Hancock Show*
Back cover still: Opening title for *Jack Hylton Presents*

Typeset in 10/11.5 pt Plantin by
D R Bungay Associates, Burghfield, Berks

Printed in Great Britain by
St Edmundsbury Press Ltd, Bury St Edmunds, Suffolk

CONTENTS

ACKNOWLEDGMENTS

The Jack Hylton collection is a remarkable one, and I should like to thank Mr R.K. Hilton for donating it to the NFTVA. I am very grateful to the following people, all of whom gave of their time to talk to me about Jack Hylton's programmes: Anthea Askey, June Whitfield, Steve Race, Alfred Marks, Paddie O'Neil, Dick Vosburgh, Brad Ashton, Peter Black, Philip Purser, Diana Parry, Erika Klausner, John P. Hamilton, Hughie Green, Bob Swash, Anne Shelton, Eric Sykes, Prof Denis McCaldin, Stella Birchington.

Thanks are also due to my colleagues at the BFI, in particular Tise Vahimagi, Dick Fiddy, Veronica Taylor, Ed Buscombe, Roma Gibson, Paul Willemen, Sue Bobbermein and Jo Barnes.

Special thanks to my colleagues at the J. Paul Getty Jnr Conservation Centre, and to Clyde Jeavons, Anne Fleming and above all Steve Bryant, without whose constant encouragement and support this book would not have been possible.

INTRODUCTION

For four and a half years after the start of Britain's first commercial television channel in September 1955, the words 'Jack Hylton Presents' heralded some of the greatest names in British variety as well as a whole host of faces which were new to television. The story of this largely forgotten piece of television history might well have been lost forever had it not been for the comprehensive archive of internal memos, letters, contracts, press cuttings and telerecordings which had been stored by the Hylton organisation in the loft of the Adelphi Theatre in London's Strand. In 1987 the Hylton interests in the Adelphi Theatre were coming to an end so the executors of the late Jack Hylton's estate entrusted the collection of television programmes and related paperwork to the care of the National Film and Television Archive.

Little was known about Jack Hylton's television career, or the programmes which were being stored in the NFTVA's vaults, but what was immediately obvious was that the films, which were mainly 35mm prints with separate magnetic soundtracks, had been stored in less than ideal conditions and as a consequence would require considerable restoration work by the NFTVA.

One immediate concern, however, was to identify the contents of the mass of cans, many of which were only labelled with working titles, and to start trying to discover programme details: correct titles, transmission dates, casts and credits. Some names, like Tony Hancock, Arthur Askey and Dickie Henderson were immediately familiar, but others, like Rosalina Neri, were virtually unknown. After viewing some of the programmes it quickly became obvious that here was a unique collection representing many of the greatest names in British Variety, which demanded detailed study.

How a man who is chiefly remembered as a band leader and theatre impresario became involved with commercial television is a fascinating story, and one that shows how commercial television fed off the variety theatre and gave very little in return. The following document explains how Hylton became involved with ITV, and why the resultant programmes came to be vilified by most of the television critics of the day.

1

Many big names in showbusiness were to regret their involvement with Jack Hylton Television Productions, but the nation has been left with a marvellous record of some of the most famous names in the variety theatre, performing routines which would otherwise exist only as a memory.

Now that ITV seems to have come full circle, with independent producers providing at least 25 per cent of programming, the story of one of ITV's earliest independents also provides a salutary lesson in what can happen when broadcasters have no control over the programmes provided for them.

1955
JACK HYLTON TAKES A BOW

Jack Hylton was an established figure in the entertainment scene of the 50s. He is best known today for his career as a band leader during the 20s and 30s. This was the heyday of the big dance bands, when people would often travel many miles to see Roy Fox, Jack Payne, or Jack Hylton. Even then Hylton had been a true showman, putting on spectacular performances with his band, and playing to enthusiastic audiences all over Europe. At the end of the Second World War Hylton had put those skills to different use, becoming a well-known and successful theatrical impresario. He had been responsible for reuniting the Crazy Gang (minus Chesney Allen) at the Victoria Palace after the war, and had interests in a wide variety of shows, from musicals like *Kiss Me Kate*, *Call Me Madam*, *Pal Joey* and *Kismet*, to revues like *Talk of the Town*. Artists like the Crazy Gang were signed exclusively to Hylton, and as he was on the board of the theatrical agents Reeves and Lamport he was in a strong position to hire talent and had many celebrities tied solely to him.

Amongst the many changes to British life in the mid-50s was the introduction of a new, commercial television channel — a rival to the monopoly of the BBC. However, rather than have just one company in opposition to the Corporation, the Conservative government of the day set up the commercial rival on a regional basis, with franchises being awarded to companies for different areas of the country. The first contract, for the London weekday franchise, was awarded on 27 October 1954, and was won by a company backed by two different organisations, Broadcast Relay Service (Rediffusion) and Lord Rothermere's Associated Newspapers, to be known as Associated-Rediffusion.

Associated-Rediffusion was in an unenviable position when it started to look seriously for its programming. The rival companies, Associated TeleVision, which held the London weekend and Midlands weekday franchise, and ABC Television, which held the Midlands and North of England weekend franchise, had on their boards men like Val Parnell and Lew Grade — entertainment giants with theatrical empires and agencies. It would have been unthinkable for A-R to deal with Moss Empires or the Grade agencies to get its light entertainment programmes, but the

3

company also knew that it would be the content of ITV's entertainment programmes that would win over viewers from the rather sedate BBC. So A-R approached Jack Hylton, the one major impresario as yet uninvolved with the new television companies. With Hylton on board they would have access to all the artists in his stable and could call on his expertise as a successful showman. On 15 July many newspapers duly reported that Jack Hylton had been contracted as Advisor on Light Entertainment. This was not unusual as A-R contracted all sorts of departmental advisors, such as Sir John Barbirolli as Music Advisor. However, some of the brief articles also mentioned that Hylton was forming his own company to make programmes exclusively for A-R, and on 30 July 1955 Jack Hylton Television Productions Ltd was duly registered, with Jack Hylton as Chairman. The objects of the company were 'to engage in and produce productions of all kinds for the purpose of television and broadcasting'.

This was an extremely canny move by Hylton, and unique in TV light entertainment at that time, although A-R was not the only company which contracted out areas of its programming. ATV contracted all its drama to H.M. Tennant, and very many of ITV's popular quiz shows were owned by independent entrepeneurs, such as Michael Miles, who owned *Take Your Pick*. Jack Hylton's contract, which was dated 13 July 1955, stated that from 26 September 1955 Jack Hylton Television Productions Ltd would supply Associated-Rediffusion with fully rehearsed productions for a period of one hour's screen time each fortnight, and a further half-hour's screen time each week. Jack Hylton Television Productions Ltd was to provide the producer, performers, costumes, scenery and props which didn't have to be specially designed and made, and the script — although A-R would be responsible for any copyright or royalty payments. The programmes were to be the best quality available for the money A-R was paying Hylton, but A-R had no jurisdiction over what Hylton provided, other than the right to ensure it fell within the requirements of the Television Act.

For Hylton, a workaholic with interests in film as well as theatre, the chance to get involved in television must have seemed a godsend. It would have appeared the perfect medium for promoting his shows and artists, and he seems to have been convinced that TV would build stars for the theatre while at the same time exploiting existing celebrities from the stage. He probably thought that with a foot in both camps he couldn't lose. He could not have foreseen that TV would sound the final death knell for variety theatre.

Hylton had less than two months to prepare his first programmes for broadcast. From the start it is obvious that the man whose instinct for a hit in the theatre had served him well, was unable to comprehend the medium of the small screen. He seems to have thought that all that was needed was to point a camera at a staged variety show, and instantly you had a TV programme. Hylton's first productions made no concessions whatsoever to what was required for a television audience.

Unfortunately, the company ran into trouble with its very first programme. Plans had been made to film acts from the Jack Hylton revue *Talk of the Town* which was playing at London's Adelphi Theatre, but Equity had called the cast out on strike. Because those being filmed did not need to rehearse their acts the union was demanding extra money to compensate for loss of rehearsal pay. The dispute was finally settled on 13 September, which left only two weeks before the first of the programmes was due to be broadcast.

Other acts were also brought in to be filmed, and sketches and songs were shot using people like Robb Wilton, Stanley Holloway, David Hughes, Hermione Gingold, Flanagan and Allen, and Jack Hylton's latest discovery, Shirley Bassey. Exactly how the first show was pieced together is not clear from the remaining component parts, but the *News Chronicle* of 29 September 1955 announced: 'Hylton's first TV variety ranges from Lauri Lane to ballerina Beryl Grey. It has been filmed in bits in London theatres and will be pieced together to look like a "live" show.'

Also billed to appear in this programme were David Hughes, Jack Tripp and Elizabeth Larner, with Flanagan and Allen topping the bill. Trying to make it look like a live show turned out to be a big mistake, however. Critics complained about the quality of the film and especially about the dubbed applause and raucous laughter. Indeed, in the *Daily Mail* of 30 September 1955 Clifford Davis wrote: 'If this is all Mr Hylton has to offer to television he should confine his activities to the live theatre — and, for pity's sake, leave television alone'. Flanagan and Allen had gone down well, but it was not an auspicious start to Hylton's TV career.

The next show to go out under the Hylton banner was *Jack Hylton's Monday Show* of 4 October 1955. It was partly studio-based, with dancers Mercedes and Triana and comedian Bernard Spear, and partly made up of film of the Spanish band leader, Xavier Cugat, shot in Paris where he and his band were appearing. Studio presentation was live and so no longer exists, but Cugat and his band introduced viewers to the new Cuban rhythm of the 'Cha Cha Cha', and his wife, Abbe Lane, added a sultry touch with her singing and dancing.

After these two programmes Hylton must have begun to have second thoughts about presenting another completely pre-recorded show, so the second variety hour was a half-and-half mix of live items and filmed sketches. The live part was hosted by David Nixon and included an interview with Italian film star Rossano Brazzi. But, paradoxically,

Hylton now began to receive adverse publicity because filmed items had been dropped in order to fit the live parts in. The main item cut was a sketch with Hermione Gingold and Henry Kendall as two old ladies on a train getting ever so slightly sozzled. They had previously performed the sketch on *The Ed Sullivan Show* in the United States, and it had been filmed for Hylton and billed for 13 October. Gingold was, to quote the *News Chronicle*, 'hopping mad about it'. The sketch was eventually included in the next of the Jack Hylton variety hours, along with Stanley Holloway and Ella Logan. Whether this programme was all filmed or part live was not reported, but Holloway's sketch and the songs of Ella Logan have survived on film.

The first of Hylton's fully live shows, and one which was to continue for a few months, was the programme *Youth Takes a Bow*. The idea behind this was that young people who were new to television would be interviewed by Bryan Michie and given a chance to show their particular talents. It was not an amateur talent show or a discoveries programme — the young people involved were all professionals — but was conceived as a way of spotlighting possible big names of the future. One of the first guests was Sandra Caron, the nineteen-year-old sister of singer Alma Cogan; others included Neville Gerard, a fifteen-year-old zoo keeper, and his penguin, Percy; guitarist Julian Bream; June Birch, a female trumpeter aged nineteen; and boy actors Andrew Ray (son of comedian Ted) and Jeremy Spenser in a specially written 'Little Lord Fauntleroy' sketch. The second edition had an equally strange mix of guests, with Lester Piggott and Shirley Bassey appearing alongside whistling page-boy Bobby Collins. It was all very worthy, but unfortunately the interviews were conducted in a rather formal fashion, with Michie sitting behind a desk and reading from his script. However, it was at least live.

Plans had already been under way for some weeks to film yet another of Hylton's stage successes, the Blackpool production of the Glenn Melvyn comedy *Love and Kisses*, starring Hylton's long-time friend Arthur Askey. This was a sequel to the play *The Love Match* which had also been produced by Hylton, and had transferred successfully to the cinema screen that year. It may well have been the relative success of this film which prompted Hylton to set up Jack Hylton Film Productions about this time, but he was obviously determined that the small screen would get *Love and Kisses*. It was to be filmed by a company called Luckwin Productions. Because Askey insisted that he had to perform before an audience, it proved cheaper to transfer the whole cast and scenery to London for a day instead of filming in the Blackpool theatre, and the play was performed before an invited audience at the Princes Theatre on Sunday, 18 October 1955. No attempt was made to adapt it for a television audience. Instead, four cameras and two sound units were set up in different parts of the theatre and the entire play was performed 'live' and recorded concurrently from different angles. Once this footage had been edited together, the play was chopped into five parts, for transmission in weekly episodes, topped and tailed by a live introduction and summary from Arthur Askey.

The plot is fairly simple and concerns Bill Brown's (Askey's) adventures after having given up his job on the railways to fulfil his ambition of running a pub. He and his friend Wally Binns will do anything to get out of actually doing any work, and at the end they somehow manage to get caught up in the local drama company's latest production, giving plenty of room for slapstick and general mayhem. Also involved were Askey's daughter, Anthea, Lally Bowers, Danny Ross, Glenn Melvyn and an actor called Bernard Graham who, as Bernard Youens, was to achieve TV immortality some years later as *Coronation Street*'s Stan Ogden.

The first 'episode' passed off without much comment in the newspapers, which were all much more interested in the Orson Welles programme on bull fighting which followed. Apparently Arthur Askey was able to work some jokes about this into his closing comments. The programme does look and sound like a stage play, with the actors projecting their voices, and a distinct lack of close-ups. Nearly forty years later it stands well as a record of an Arthur Askey stage play but as Jack Hylton's first situation comedy it has to be given the thumbs down, even though there are understandable reasons for filming a stage play like this — lack of time to create a five-week series from scratch being the main one.

By this time, the one-hour variety shows were fully live, and compered by the American master of ceremonies, George Jessel. The programme of 24 November was notable for Jessel being the only male in an otherwise all-female line up which ran from Vera Lynn to Sabrina to the Luton Girls' Choir. Again, these shows were full variety bills with no concessions made to a television audience. It was the first time that TV audiences had heard Sabrina sing, however, and the girl who had become famous by staying silent appeared in a sketch called 'Housewives' Choice' taken from the Crazy Gang's current revue, *Jokers Wild*.

The programmes produced by Jack Hylton for the rest of the year continued along much the same lines, with *Love and Kisses* drawing to a close, and *Youth Takes a Bow* continuing fortnightly in addition to the fortnightly hour of variety. Half-hour variety programmes entitled *Jack Hylton Presents* came from Hylton's Albany Club at Hylton House on Saville Row, which he bought at the end of November. For Christmas, Hylton was able to promote his Streatham Hill Theatre pantomime,

Babes in the Wood with Arthur Askey, by televising excerpts on 23 December. Whether Hylton himself considered that he had a successful start to his TV career is not recorded, but after his seasonal variety offering of 22 December, Peter Black wrote in the *Daily Mail* of 23rd December:

> Has Jack Hylton the slightest idea of the standard of programme that is being presented on ITV under his name? ... Mr Hylton does his reputation no good with such stuff.
>
> Programmes such as [*Jack Hylton Presents*] and the recent Askey series in which a two-hour play was filmed and arbitrarily chopped into five weekly parts, and last week's inept show from the Albany Club, suggest that Mr Hylton is treating TV less as an audience in its own right than as suitable receptive material for plugs of his contract artists.

It was not an auspicious end to 1955 for Hylton: the final reviews of the year complained about the numbers of plugs made by those appearing in the shows from the Albany Club, and of course these were mainly plugs for Jack Hylton artists in Jack Hylton shows at Jack Hylton theatres. However, there were to be new names and new series for 1956, and the ITV audience, initially confined to the Midlands and the South of England, was growing all the time.

CHANNEL 24
PROVIDES A HIT FOR HYLTON

At the start of 1956 Hylton had an interest in ten shows running in the West End and 1,200 artists on his payroll. His foray into TV had not been considered a success by critics, although *Jack Hylton Presents* was constantly in the TAM Top Ten. James Thomas, writing in the *News Chronicle* of 19 January, probably summed up the critics' views at that time:

> Mr Hylton's shows, which cost ITV a sizeable chunk of its overdraft, have produced among them a few which have reached a new low in TV light entertainment. So badly presented, so clearly under-rehearsed have some of them seemed to be, that Mr Hylton could only ask himself what the new excursion can do for his reputation. ... The Hylton hours and half-hours remain the mainstays of midweek ITV variety. Soon they may reach a slightly astonished provincial audience. Mr Hylton, not before time, has decided to act.

Hylton had decided to make some changes to his television output by making the hourly programmes more than just straight variety bills. The first of these was a vehicle for Max Miller, called *You'd Never Believe It*. Miller was sixty-one and famous as the 'cheeky chappie' master of the blue joke and suggestive ditty. To tone him down for television inevitably meant that his act was less successful.

Youth Takes a Bow continued, with the first programme of 1956 including Jim Dale, who had just completed his National Service in the RAF. The Friday night half-hour of entertainment came from the Albany Club, which Hylton was running as a normal nightclub and which was always full of his showbusiness friends and colleagues. The show on 27 January marked the television debut of a young Italian lady who was to play an important role in Jack Hylton's private and public life.

Rosalina Neri had been 'discovered' by Hylton on a visit to Italy. Dubbed 'Italy's Marilyn Monroe' she was blonde and sexy, with a very curvaceous figure. The press stories said that the twenty-four-year-old had ambitions to be an opera singer and had been banned from Italian

9

TV for being too sexy, but her talent and her grasp of English were very limited. She became the main woman in Hylton's life, and he was obviously determined to launch her career in England. This sort of patronage was, of course, not unusual in those days, but he does seem to have been blind to her lack of talent and was to try very hard to create television vehicles for her during the next four years.

The second new show in January 1956 was an attempt to create a programme like *The Ed Sullivan Show* in America, but based around newspaper columnist Arthur Helliwell. His column in the *People* was popular, and Helliwell's trilby hat, or 'titfer', had become his trademark. Hylton supposedly gave Helliwell control of his choice of guests, although he remained as an advisor on the programme. It was an astute piece of work on Hylton's part; he must have realised that the link with a newspaper would mean a great deal of valuable free publicity, not only for the programme but also for the acts featured in it. *The Arthur Helliwell Show* drew this response from Peter Black in the *Daily Mail* of January 31:

> I can think of only three ways in which he [Helliwell] could improve. He could decide whether he will speak English or American, could improve his script, which at times was barely intelligible, and could think of something to do with his hat other than wear it at a rakish angle.

Helliwell's next column in the *People* of 5 February 1956 contained a detailed account of the chaos that had surrounded him during the full day of rehearsals preceding that first night's show. It's difficult to believe Helliwell's report that he hadn't even set foot in the studio until thirteen hours before live transmission, and none of the acts had been rehearsed, but he assures his readers that:

> I'm still convinced that it's plain lunacy to expect to put on a good show after keeping your cast hanging around all day. They tell me that the same thing happens with almost every new commercial programme. If this is true, then I am not in the least surprised by the deplorable quality of much of the 'entertainment' inflicted on the unfortunate viewers.

Apparently the only calm presence around was Jack Hylton himself, who kept materialising in clouds of cigar smoke and assuring Helliwell: 'Don't worry, Arthur. It'll be all right on the night'.

That same day, 5 February, the *Sunday Graphic* had a full-page article by Ken Passingham based on an interview with Hylton.

Passingham had wanted to find out why the shows were so poor and contained so many plugs for other Hylton interests. Hylton is quoted as saying:

> Maybe I began too soon — at a time when the people I would have liked to put on television were tied down in the theatre. I am changing that. I've had to wait for Arthur Askey, for example. Al Read is another. Shani Wallis another. I won't book them into the theatre again until I get them on television.

Cheekily, Hylton was using film of some of the acts which he had recorded in 1955 to fill out spots in *The Arthur Helliwell Show*, as paperwork in the collection states that Frank Muir and Denis Norden's 'Lighthouse' sketch, filmed at the Adelphi Theatre on 14 September 1955 and starring Tony Hancock, was used in the programme transmitted on 6 February 1956. The filmed sketch is in the NFTVA's safe keeping but, sadly, has no sound.

The second week of February saw the next of Hylton's new series. The successful BBC comedy programme *Before Your Very Eyes* was transferred — lock, stock and Sabrina — to Channel 9. It was this sketch show, scripted by Sid Colin and Talbot Rothwell, which the previous year had turned a silent blonde named Norma Sykes into a national celebrity as the pneumatic Sabrina. Advance publicity played on the fact that Sabrina would sing and act in the new show — she had been taking acting, elocution and singing lessons. The programme was, of course, a vehicle for Arthur Askey, popular comedian and friend of Hylton. Although the first edition was not recorded, it can be assumed that Askey was not entirely happy with it as Peter Black reports that the programme 'did not show the little man at his best. At the end he came forward and explained that the second edition would be better.' This would not be the last time that Askey apologised for a Hylton programme, and he would not be the only artist to apologise to the viewers for the quality of the previous week's show.

One of the few series to be a critical as well as a popular success, began on Thursday 16 February 1956 as an experimental replacement for a last minute cancellation. Copyright problems with a variety programme which director Douglas Hurn had been planning meant that the show had been pulled at a very late stage. Hurn rang Alfred Marks to see if he would be able to help out with a replacement programme. Marks had been compering some of Hylton's shows from the Albany Club and was eager to do something different from the normal run-of-the-mill variety programme. He was also keen to be seen as an actor rather than a comedian.

11

Alfred Marks and his wife, Paddie O'Neil, remember well that it was Paddie who took Hurn's call, and, thinking on her feet, she immediately suggested an idea. Some time before, Paddie had seen a magazine cover with a picture of Ex-RSM Brittain, who had been the most senior RSM in the British Army, and she promptly thought of having him open the programme by barking out the command: 'Alfred Marks Time'. Alfred Marks would then be seen taking a phone call asking him what he would do if he had to provide a last minute programme for the fictional Channel Twenty-Four. He would then begin to explain what viewers would see, and the entertainment would start, then at the end he would explain why, in actual fact, the viewers wouldn't be seeing this on their TV screens.

For writers, Paddie immediately thought of Dick Vosburgh and Brad Ashton, who had written for Marks's BBC radio programme *The Show Band Show*; she herself would also devise sketches and write scripts (although she was never publicly credited). The idea was to have something which would stand out as original and entertaining. Alfred Marks insisted that there should be no dancers or speciality acts, and that the writers were to write comic sketches for straight actors, not comedians.

Ex-RSM Brittain introduces an episode of *Alfred Marks Time*

The one-off programme proved so successful it was immediately commissioned as a series, but it was to be a monthly rather than weekly or fortnightly programme. This meant that the writers would have two weeks to write material and then the company would have ten days for rehearsal. Much of *Alfred Marks Time*'s appeal lay in the fact that the audience never knew who was going to pop up next in a sketch with Marks and O'Neil. It was also one of the first programmes to make fun of other TV shows and commercials — with the added bonus of having guests from the very programmes it was spoofing. Alan Wheatley played the Sheriff of Nottingham in a spoof of *The Adventures of Robin Hood*, and Edmund Purdom appeared in a satire of *Sword of Freedom*. Dulcie Gray appeared in a skit on the legal series *Boyd QC* which starred her husband, Michael Denison, and Peter Sellers appeared as Ralph Reader, in an impression so uncannily accurate that when the real Ralph Reader appeared in the next series some viewers complained that he wasn't as good as he had been first time around. Many other actors appeared in sketches, including Bernard Miles and Shirley Eaton, and in fact *Alfred Marks Time* was very much the *Morecambe and Wise Show* of its day.

Although the actors appearing in sketches were 'straight' actors, comedians and other personalities also turned up on the programme delivering punchlines to sketches, usually appearing for only a few seconds. Band leader Edmundo Ros appeared as a bus conductor in one sketch, quizmaster Hughie Green appeared in another, and people like Max Wall, Max Bygraves, Terry-Thomas, and even the great Max Miller were happy to turn up and deliver only a few words. Writer Dick Vosburgh recalls that the second time Miller was hired to deliver a punchline he insisted on doing a routine, much to the delight of the rather bemused audience. Songs were provided by Alfred Marks, who possessed a very fine, operatically trained voice, and Ray Ellington, who would usually sing with Paddie O'Neil.

Alfred Marks Time soon became a great favourite with audience and critics alike. The monthly visit to Channel Twenty-Four was the highlight of Hylton's programming for A-R. After the second show, Philip Purser wrote in the *Daily Mail* of 16 March 1956: 'On ITV *Alfred Marks Time* was a minor revelation: a light entertainment which kept going for 60 minutes without noticeably flagging. This is an achievement which few of its brethren half that length can manage.' At last Jack Hylton had something that could be termed a hit. In the meantime the Friday night series *Jack Hylton Presents* was still being broadcast from The Albany Club, and *The Arthur Helliwell Show* and *Before Your Very Eyes* continued their runs.

March saw the first episode of a series called *I'm Not Bothered* which had been devised by Glenn Melvyn, writer and co-star of *Love and*

Kisses. He reprised his character Wally Binns, and Danny Ross was once again Alf Hall. Melvyn was not the only writer working on this: Edward J. Mason, a scriptwriter from BBC Radio series *The Archers*, wrote the first episode, and others were written by Patrick Brawn, Max Kester, Cecelia Hale and Edward Dryhurst. *I'm Not Bothered* was not very well received. Philip Purser wrote in the *Daily Mail* of 3 March 1956:

> In its relentless search for mediocrity television light entertainment can never afford to relinquish the formula which has already proved successfully awful.
>
> Glenn Melvyn's farce *Love and Kisses*, sawn up into five or six spasms, was (in the face of extensive competition) quite one of the most dreadful shows of 1955. What more natural then, that Mr Melvyn should be encouraged to return to the screen as soon as possible with another episodic comedy, launched on London ITV last night. ... It can be summed up by an illustration from the first few moments: A man with toothache is funny: a man shouting is funny: ergo a shouting man with toothache is a real scream.

Although never recorded, and forgotten by most people, one episode in particular would be fascinating to look at now. The episode transmitted on 8 May 1956 was written by Glenn Melvyn and contained the first TV appearance by Ronnie Barker. Barker writes in his autobiography, *It's Hello From Him*, that not only did Melvyn give him his television debut, but he also let him ghost-write the episode. While appearing in repertory theatre with Melvyn, Barker had learned to stutter, much like Melvyn's character Wally Binns, and was to use this knowledge when creating the character of Arkwright in *Open All Hours*. 'Ronald Barker' also appeared in the episode which went out on 29 May, and his contract shows that he was paid £10 plus two guineas per day for rehearsals.

Although *I'm Not Bothered* was initially commissioned for six episodes, it was to continue for twenty-six. The Hylton organisation hoped that it would continue further, but A-R felt that the ratings were not sufficiently high enough to interest the advertisers and it was dropped after the run ended.

March also saw a one-off half-hour special starring Doretta Morrow. The programme itself went unremarked, but it appears to have caused something of a panic at Jack Hylton Television Productions because when Morrow returned to New York, she accidentally took with her a dress that had been specially made for the programme. It seems that A-R were responsible for paying for the costume but wouldn't pay for something which was now on the other side of the Atlantic.

In April 1956 the big event for the Hylton organisation was the televising of the Crazy Gang. Jack Hylton had been producing the Crazy Gang revues at the Victoria Palace since the end of the war, and these venerable old gentlemen were something of an English institution. Their revues were immensely popular, bawdy, knock-about comedy which had been filling the theatre night after night for years. It must have been quite a coup to produce their first live television performance.

Most of the sketches and music routines were from their current show at the Victoria Palace, *Jokers Wild*, which had been running since December 1954. Although the live show wasn't recorded, the paperwork in the NFTVA's collection gives a good idea of what was in the programme. There were song and dance routines from the *Jokers Wild* company and the Tiller Girls, plus the Gang in crossover routines, a teddyboy dance routine and a sketch based on *The Scarlet Pimpernel*. Whilst the live performances have been lost, the routines were filmed later that year for another programme, *Friday Night with the Crazy Gang*, which has survived.

A second programme of excerpts from *Jokers Wild* was transmitted on 24 May, but this show was filmed the day before. It is probably the closest a modern audience will ever get to seeing the stage antics which had made the Crazy Gang so popular. It was filmed in front of a live audience and, while it may not stand up as a TV programme, being described by James Thomas in the *News Chronicle* of 31 May 1956 as 'badly lit, sloppily cut filming', as a record of a Crazy Gang revue it has enormous historical value. Above all, it conveys something of the anarchy and energy that made the Gang such a phenomenal success.

Just three days after the Crazy Gang's first television show, Hylton was to transfer another big name to television, although this artist had yet to reach the height of his fame. Tony Hancock was developing a huge following for his radio show *Hancock's Half Hour*, which would soon transfer successfully to BBC Television. He had been appearing in a Jack Hylton revue at the Adelphi theatre called *The Talk of the Town*, but had tired of doing the same routines over and again every night and had finally gone AWOL from the show. In order to prevent Hylton holding him to his contract for *The Talk of the Town*, Hancock had to agree to doing two series for ITV.

Called simply *The Tony Hancock Show* it began on 27 April, co-starred June Whitfield, and was scripted by Eric Sykes. Sykes had been in New York with Max Bygraves when he received a cable from Jack Hylton asking if he could write for Tony Hancock for television. He had already written for Hancock in his role as the tutor in the radio series *Educating Archie*. Sykes considered Hylton's cable too vague and said so in his reply, but on his return to England, Hylton telephoned him immediately to ask him again. Sykes eventually agreed and the resultant shows were transmitted live, but were also telerecorded. The format was different to that of Hancock's BBC series as the programmes consisted of sketches, broken up by a song from June Whitfield and a dance routine by The Teenagers in order to give Hancock time to change his costume for the next sketch.

The first programme was not particularly well reviewed and indeed Hancock seems to have been aware of this as he apologises for the fact at the beginning of the second one and says he hopes they will do better this week. James Thomas wrote in the *News Chronicle* of 28 April: 'Hancock was by no means as funny as he is on the radio. The show looked slackly presented, relying too much for its humour on carefully conceived "mistakes".' However, as the series progressed the programmes got better, with quite sophisticated running-jokes. Eric Sykes recollects that he wrote the series from week to week, so was able to write for the strengths of the actors and allow the characters to grow and develop.

The Tony Hancock Show and *I'm Not Bothered* continued to run throughout May and June, with further instalments of *Alfred Marks Time* every month. Hylton was then able to announce a series of shows

Hancock conducts the Last Night of the Proms in *The Tony Hancock Show*

starring the great Scottish actor, singer and dancer Jack Buchanan as the host of Mayfair's Twenty-One Club. Hylton also televised excerpts from two of his theatre shows — Buchanan in his old stage success *Castles in the Air*, and *Me and My Girl* starring Lauri Lupino Lane, son of Lupino Lane.

In July, the benefit to Hylton of telerecording some of his programmes became obvious when, on 10 July, he repeated an earlier edition of *Before Your Very Eyes* which had originally gone out live on 9 March. Contracts in the collection makes it clear that the repeat date had already been fixed at the time of the first transmission. The NFTVA holds the original live programme and the 'repeat', which simply has Askey's reference to *Idiot Weekly* (a programme that had followed the earlier March transmission) cut out. The programme on 17 July had initially been transmitted on 6 April, and the programme on 24 July was also a repeat.

July also saw a new series appearing under the Hylton banner, *My Husband and I*, which was created as a vehicle for Evelyn 'Boo' Laye and her husband, Frank Lawton, after her successful guest appearance on Max Miller's *You'd Never Believe It*. Described as a domestic comedy, it was really just an excuse to showcase Laye and appears to have been rather 'precious', showing the ups and downs of life for a typical West End couple. Preliminary suggestions for episodes included such exciting situations as: 'buying a hat; changing the car; growing a moustache; guest coming to stay; guest who never goes; new dress unnoticed; buying on the HP'. (*My Husband and I* file, Hylton collection.) Peter Black wrote in *The Daily Mail* of 18 August: 'Miss Laye's comedy style, suggesting a blend of Queen Victoria and Gertrude Lawrence struggling against the effects of a glass of cowslip wine at a hot garden party, catches perfectly the appeal of both'.

The series of six was given an extension of one week, but plans to do a follow-up series with the Bradens (Bernard Braden and Barbara Kelly) and their children never really got off the ground. Miss Laye was given a costume allowance of £250 for the initial six programmes, to be paid for by A-R, but as she spent over double that amount the remaining costs had to be picked up by Jack Hylton.

Also that month, Hylton was able to persuade comedian Al Read to do a one-off special for him based on the show called *Such is Life* which he was appearing in at the Adelphi Theatre.

In August a musical play called *The Lilac Domino* was adapted for television presentation, and a new Friday night series of cabaret shows presented by Terry-Thomas began. These were given the inspired title *Friday Night* and guests included Hutch, Terence Morgan, Leslie Mitchell, Adelaide Hall and Michael Bentine. However, James

Thomas wrote in the *News Chronicle* of 11 August: 'Poor Terry-Thomas, billed in his own show for the first time on ITV, found himself heaved into the usual Channel 9 predicament of merely having to compere a not very bright variety show'.

August was also supposed to see the TV presentation of another musical play, *The Straker Special*, in which June Whitfield would star as a female mechanic, with Dennis Quilley. (The 'Straker Special' was a car.) However, June Whitfield developed appendicitis, so the show had to be postponed.

September saw the continuation of *My Husband and I*, *I'm Not Bothered* and *Friday Night*, with further antics from the Crazy Gang and another presentation of one of Hylton's West End musicals from the 1930s, *Twenty To One*, starring Lupino Lane. This was also the month in which the Crazy Gang were networked for the first time, having appeared only in the London region for their previous shows. They achieved the biggest TAM ratings of the year, with a massive 82 per cent of TV sets tuned to their show in the London region. Their half-hour show was seen in 1,399,000 homes, the largest audience since the start of ITV, which gives some indication of their popularity.

The first of the Crazy Gang shows for October, *Friday Night with the Crazy Gang*, was, for some reason, filmed. This is the one which contains

The Crazy Gang in an extract from *A Midsummer Night's Dream* in *The Music Box*

the sketches which went out in the first live show in April, although the feel of a live stage performance is completely lost as the laughter and applause are obviously dubbed. Some of the camera angles are rather strange, and considering that they were not constrained by the presence of an audience, rather a lot of the action happens off-camera. Guest critic Nicholas Monsarrat wrote in the *Evening Standard* of 6 October:

> Among the most admirable qualities of the British is loyalty; but when it extends to these five old gentlemen lumbering through a routine which really wrung its last involuntary laugh a full 20 years ago, I really think loyalty can be stretched too far.

The following week's show received better reviews, perhaps because it was live. An interesting point to note is that the NFTVA collection also has a short piece of cine film of the 'Tedwardian Nights' routine from this programme, with the Gang all dressed in different coloured teddyboy outfits. It is shot mainly from the wings, but also from front of stage, and is in colour, giving it an immediacy and vibrancy which is sadly missing from the finished programme. It may well be the only colour film record of the Crazy Gang in action on stage.

Alfred Marks Time also returned in October for a regular monthly slot, while *My Husband and I* drew to a close. The first of an occasional series of programmes featuring the Lady Ratlings was also broadcast that month. The Lady Ratlings were a charitable organisation which had been set up in 1929 as the female equivalent of the variety profession's all-male Grand Order of Water Rats. Members of the 'lodge' were either wives of Water Rats or variety performers in their own right. The highlight of the Ratlings's year was the October Annual Dinner and Ball, during which the floor show was provided by members. It was this floor show that Hylton decided to transfer to the TV screen, no doubt because in May the BBC had broadcast the Water Rats in a revue called *Rats To You*, which starred Max Bygraves, Peter Brough and Archie Andrews, Davy Kaye and Cardew Robinson.

The review in the *Stage* of 1 November gives a detailed listing of all the acts and performers for the Lady Ratlings cabaret, which included Doris Hare, Anne (Bud) Flanagan, Ivy Benson, and Dorita (Charlie) Chester. It reads like a good old-fashioned (and all-female) variety bill, with songs, music hall turns, dances and comedy, the final act being: 'A competition between the old and new styles in entertainment, covering sister acts, male impersonators, chorus singers, dancing acts and other departments, ranging from clog dancing to rock 'n' roll'.

In November the *Friday Night* shows were back, with Tommy Trinder as compere, but the programmes no longer came from The Albany Club, which had now closed. Instead, A-R's Wembley studios had been done up to look like a night club, and Trinder and his star guest, the French singer Patachou, performed in front of thirty extras in evening dress sitting at tables. Also returning was *Before Your Very Eyes* with Arthur Askey, which alternated weekly with a new series of *The Tony Hancock Show*. This new Hancock series was to be different from his first for Jack Hylton, with no singing or dancing, and only one storyline. Scripts were credited to Associated London Scripts Ltd but the programmes started off unsuccessfully and in order to save the series Ray Galton and Alan Simpson, the writers of Hancock's BBC radio and television series, were asked to step in. Since they were already contracted to the BBC, they were unable to receive any credit for their scripts.

Although the first in the series didn't receive tremendous acclaim, some further episodes were deemed more worthy of Hancock's talents. In general, though, Hancock's brief period on ITV didn't do his reputation a great deal of good. It is interesting to note, however, that the style of the programmes changed. A report of the third programme says that it was virtually a solo performance with Hancock satirising a Hollywood travelogue, impersonating Charles Laughton, pretending to be an American swoon singer. It sounds remarkably like the infamous one-man-show at the Royal Festival Hall in which his promised new material turned out to be Hancock going through all his old routines.

The Straker Special finally made it to the screen, with June Whitfield as a singing and dancing mechanic and Dennis Quilley as the owner of the fabulous car on which the musical was based. It didn't exactly set the screen alight. Bernard Levin wrote in the *Manchester Guardian* of 24 November 1956: 'Book and lyrics were lame with that peculiarly amateur lameness that is the hall-mark of undergraduate musicals, and the music was wishy-washy in the extreme'. But June Whitfield got her usual good reviews.

For the last month of 1956, *The Tony Hancock Show* alternated with *Before Your Very Eyes*, and there was another monthly outing for *Alfred Marks Time*. Hylton's big plans for Christmas were a TV version of Arthur Askey's pantomime from the Golders Green Hippodrome, and a live variety special. The panto was *Humpty Dumpty*, with Askey as the Dame, Clara Crumpet, and his daughter Anthea as Humpty Dumpty. Also in the cast were Lauri Lupino Lane and George Truzzi, with Maggie Fitzgibbon as the Principal Boy. The *News Chronicle* offered members of its children's Redskins Club the chance to be in the audience for the live performance so presumably the theatre was full of happy little Indian braves that night. However, for contractual reasons only forty minutes of the pantomime could be shown — the rest of the time had to be filled in with other variety acts which were not appearing in *Humpty Dumpty*. The programme also visited Arthur Askey in his dressing room, where he was interviewed by McDonald Hobley. Apparently his ad libbing skills were also called into play when part of the scenery wall behind him fell down.

Christmas Greetings was a seasonal variety programme, introduced by Dickie Henderson, which included a French singer called Phillipe Clay, two juggling Spanish brothers and the ubiquitous Rosalina Neri. Philip Phillips wrote in the *Daily Herald* of 22 December 1956:

> I thought that Rosalina Neri, the blond Italian, was going to collapse last night from exhaustion in her efforts to be sexy in ITV's *Christmas Greetings* show. She pouted, wriggled and ogled so much that she seemed like a combination of Sabrina, the young Marlene Dietrich and Marilyn Monroe — but grown to nightmare proportions. Please Miss Neri, more restraint — or you'll have us laughing.

On 23 December, ABC treated viewers in the Midlands to the full-length version of *Love and Kisses*, which ran for two hours. It was no more successful in this format than it had been as five episodes, but at least Askey didn't have to come on beforehand and explain to the viewers what was going on.

And so Jack Hylton TV Productions' first full year drew to a close with the fourth of Tony Hancock's shows. In terms of viewing figures it had been a great success, with *Jack Hylton Presents* consistently in the Top Ten TAM and Nielsen ratings. The viewing public were tuning in in large numbers to see their favourite comedians. On a critical level, however, the programmes produced in his name had been less successful. ITV was beginning to change the shape of British broadcasting and was also changing the way people viewed TV, even though less than a third of the BBC's audience could receive it. The commercial channel's news programmes were pacier and more informal than the BBC's and the Corporation was already starting to react to this. Drama, too, was already becoming one of ITV's strengths. But the real impact on the viewers came from the quiz shows: *Take Your Pick* and *Double Your Money* fast became big audience pullers, turning Michael Miles and Hughie Green into household names. The BBC was still broadcasting old favourites like *What's My Line,* but ITV's quiz shows not only had audience participation, they also had big cash prizes for the winners.

It was therefore strange that light entertainment was still so bogged-down with variety, no programmes more so than those produced by Hylton. Intimate cabaret revues and variety fare did not (and still do not) transfer well to a TV screen. There was no imagination involved and no attempt to be innovative. Many of the artists featured on Jack

Hylton programmes were appearing in shows in which Hylton had an interest and there seems to have been a tendency to feature those people appearing at Hylton theatres rather than specifically seeking out acts suited to television.

Not that the BBC was immune from this criticism. The Corporation's radio programmes often seem much more interesting and adventurous than its TV ones, with plenty of music and variety on both the Home Service and Light Programme. However, on its television channel the BBC was offering viewers *The Billy Cotton Band Show* and *Come Dancing,* as well as *Whack-O* and *Great Scott It's Maynard* with Terry Scott and Bill Maynard.

With hindsight, one can look back on 1956 and see that certain programmes would have enormous influence on future generations. Spike Milligan's *A Show Called Fred* probably changed TV comedy for ever, paving the way for *It's a Square World, At Last the 1948 Show, Monty Python's Flying Circus* and all subsequent surreal comedy. It shone amidst a sea of mediocrity even then.

It is incredible to think of the great comic actor Tony Hancock doing three series within the space of eight months. Yet that great genius was stuck without the equally great talents of Ray Galton and Alan Simpson. A more simple way of putting it would be that in 1956 Jack Hylton wasted the talents of a great many people. Arthur Askey's humour does not appeal to everyone, but there can be no denying his skill and experience in front of the TV cameras. Paddie O'Neil was not allowed a credit for devising and writing *Alfred Marks Time,* while Rosalina Neri was wiggling her way through guest appearances in various shows. So, though Hylton's first full year as an independent television producer was a success in terms of audience viewing figures, he must have known that all was not rosy and that there would have to be some changes to the quality of the programming he provided during 1957.

THE WOOLWORTH AUDIENCE

Jack Hylton's first programme for 1957 was *Alfred Marks Time*, and this was followed by another in the series *Friday Night*, although the programme's 'on screen' title was *Music Box*. The *TV Times* credits the host of the show as Dickie Henderson, but it was, in fact, Tommy Trinder. This particular show is just about the most shameless advertisement for Hylton's theatrical interests in the whole of the Hylton collection. The French singer Patachou was appearing at the Adelphi Theatre, as were George Tapps and his dancers and Tommy Trinder. Jean Wynser was appearing at the Victoria Palace, and Trinder made sure that she got in a good plug for the Crazy Gang show which was also playing there. Even the 'boys and girls' of the company were from the Adelphi Theatre. Such blatant self-promotion might almost have been

An almost unrecognisable Tommy Trinder in *The Music Box*

forgivable if the resulting show had been good, but it is a strange mish-mash which looks as if it was thrown together in a hurry. The opening dance number seems to go on forever, and the comedy sketch which closes the first half is unfunny in the extreme.

The most bizarre aspect of the whole show, however, is Tommy Trinder's performance. In an item at the end of the show called 'Music Hall Memories', Trinder first appears as Harry Champion, singing 'Any Old Iron' and then, for reasons which are never explained, he appears in drag, dresssed as what appears to be a pantomime principal boy, singing 'Strolling Down the Strand With a Banana in My Hand'. It is a strange and wonderful sight, but seems to have nothing to do with the music hall. The plugs obviously didn't go unnoticed; as a letter from an 'entertainment producer' in the *Advertisers Weekly* of 11 January said:

> An advertiser was presenting his own show. The show advertised his products and, more to the point, his products or artists were adver-tising him. Tommy Trinder, for example, had to bring into his rep-artee that he was appearing at the Adelphi. ... In all, I would say it was first-class advertising for the great J. H. Organisation.

Viewers hadn't seen the last of the special versions of Hylton musical plays: *Balalaika* was the first offering for 1957. The book and lyrics were by Eric Maschwitz, and George Posford, composer of 'Goodnight Vienna', wrote the music. Dick Bentley was the star of this pre-war musical about Russian emigrés in a Paris restaurant, along with Donald Scott, Betty Paul and Patricia Bredin. Peter Black in the *Daily Mail* of 18 January 1957 called it: 'as silly an entertainment as 1957 is likely to offer'. This is not really surprising when a three-and-a-quarter-hour musical had to be reduced to fifty-one minutes in order to fit into a TV slot that required twenty-five minutes of dialogue and twenty-five of music. It suffered because of this, but it also suffered for being old-fashioned and rather irrelevant to a 1957 audience.

The next edition of *The Music Box* was advertised as such, and starred Bud Flanagan and Ivy Benson and her band, plus a singer and dancers from the latest Crazy Gang show at the Victoria Palace. It also contained an excellent example of 'Monsewer' Eddie Gray's juggling act.

For *The Music Box* on 1 February Bud Flanagan was back again, but this time with the rest of the Crazy Gang. They appeared in a sketch from *These Foolish Kings*, their latest revue at the Victoria Palace. It was not the usual type of sketch, however, but an excerpt from *A Mid-summer Night's Dream*, the 'most lamentable comedy of Pyramus and Thisbe'. It took up the whole of the second part of the programme and was played 'straight'. The first part of the programme was the usual variety bill, with a singer, dancers, a comedy whistling act and Rosalina Neri. The following week Terry-Thomas hosted the show, as well as performing in a sketch with Leslie Mitchell and singing a rather strange and unintelligible song.

February 14 brought another TV version of a formerly successful West End musical comedy. This time it was Noel Gay's *Sweetheart Mine*, the story of two cockney greengrocers, which became *'Appy as 'Arry* starring Lupino Lane and Lauri Lupino Lane. (It also had an appearance from a sixteen-year-old Anthony Valentine.) It was the first time that father and son appeared together on TV, so it is a shame that the show was not recorded. Kenneth Bell wrote in the *Manchester Evening Chronicle*:

> Every situation was grossly overplayed, the plot was negligible, and the comedy, oddly flavoured by drips of sentimentality, was laid on with a steam shovel. The really remarkable thing is that a man of Jack Hylton's discernment should be responsible for presenting such rubbish.

The following night's edition of *Music Box* was hosted by Leslie Sarony. The first part of the programme was fairly straightforward, with a pair of dancers and a songstress, but the second half was much more interesting. After telling a few jokes, Sarony introduced a young girl whom he said would go far, but this young girl turned out to be Tommy Trinder in drag singing 'Strolling Down the Strand', which Sarony then finished singing and claimed to have written for Trinder. The clip of Trinder was actually from the programme transmitted six weeks earlier, but no attempt was made to explain that. Sarony could have asked the audience if they remembered it and explained that he wrote it, instead they were asked to believe that Trinder was actually appearing. The closing act was Max Miller, in an outrageous flowery suit and hat, who sang some songs and told a few slightly risqué stories.

The final show in this series was actually two weeks later, and was remarkable for having a dance performance from the American actor George Raft. The publicised star, George Formby, had cancelled all engagements because of laryngitis, so Raft, who had danced with Jack Hylton's band many years earlier in 1926, stepped in to fill the gap as a favour. It was his first appearance on British TV and looking at his dance routine you can't help thinking that it must have been some favour he owed Jack Hylton.

The previous Friday saw the start of a short series which can still hold its own today. *La Plume de ma Tante* was a saucy French review

George Raft steps out for Hylton after stepping-in for George Formby in *The Music Box*

which Hylton had been presenting at the Garrick Theatre for fifteen months, and which had become something of a cult. The show's writer, co-director and star, Robert Dhéry, had introduced a new sort of comedy to the English, and there was also some nudity in it. Hylton had bought a lot of Dhéry's material for the Crazy Gang revue *Jokers Wild*, including what became 'Tedwardian Nights' and 'Freres Jacques', a sketch with bell-ringing monks. The televised excerpts were called *The Robert Dhéry Show* and, while they were obviously toned down and some of the sketches which had been deemed unsuitable had been cut, the general flavour of the show came across very well on television. The programmes were recorded at A-R's Wembley television studios, which does cramp some of the sketches, but the skill of Dhéry's troupe and their expertise, after having performed the sketches for over a year, meant that *The Robert Dhéry Show* not only provided something different from the normal fare of the day, it also stands up to modern-day scrutiny.

Alfred Marks Time continued its monthly appearances, with James Thomas writing in the *News Chronicle* of 1 March:

On ITV, Alfred Marks rescued Jack Hylton Productions from the doldrums with a comedy show crammed with ideas and personalities. ... [Marks] has the sense not to turn up week by week wearing out his welcome with desperate material.

Marks made a second TV appearance that month when he starred in an adaptation of the musical *High Button Shoes,* in which he had made his name in 1949 when it was produced by Jack Hylton at the London Hippodrome. The part had originally been written for Phil Silvers, and the original London production had the young Audrey Hepburn in the chorus.

Another special with the Lady Ratlings was broadcast that month, and was followed by Jack Hylton's tribute to Arthur Askey's thirty years in show business, *Arthur's Anniversary.* Many of the newspapers had billed it in advance as a big celebration, with the cream of showbusiness turning up for it. Askey even made the cover of that week's *TV Times,* but it was a very disappointing show and a huge let-down for a much-loved comedian.

In April, the Jack Hylton publicity machine swung into action well before transmission to announce that Bud Flanagan was being re-united with his former partner, Chesney Allen, for a series of six programmes in which they would sing some of the songs they had made famous, as well as performing their old comic sketches. Flanagan was appearing

Flanagan (right) and Allen, re-united for *Together Again*

twice-nightly in the Crazy Gang's latest revue, *These Foolish Kings*, while Allen had retired from the Crazy Gang in 1946 owing to ill-health and had become a theatrical agent. He was a director of Reeves and Lamport, as was Jack Hylton. Hylton obviously knew that there was no chance of them performing together on stage again but a pre-recorded programme would still be possible and would be enormously popular with the public. The series, called *Together Again*, proved to be a real feast of nostalgia, with plenty of the duo's well-known songs and sketches. It was all familiar material but no less popular for all that. Indeed, it stands today as a good record of some of their most famous routines.

April was obviously nostalgia month for Hylton as he revived another successful partnership, that of Richard Murdoch and Arthur Askey in the pre-war radio series *Band Waggon*, except that this time their flat was not on top of Broadcasting House but A-R's Television House, and the programme was called *Living It Up*. The idea behind the programme was exactly the same as the old radio series and the critical reaction was generally favourable. The one surviving episode from this series is rather manic and could just as easily have been done on the radio. Viewers were presumably supposed to be familiar with *Band Waggon* and thus were expected to pick up a lot of the references to characters and previous storylines.

There was also room for newer talent, however, in a special billed in the *TV Times* as 'a kaleidoscope of light entertainment' in which more established names like Joan Sims and Peter Butterworth were joined by newer artists who had been 'spotted' by director Douglas Hurn, either on other television shows or on the stage. 'Plenty of zip' was one reviewer's comment about the programme *Spring Fling*.

The Lady Ratlings returned again for a May show, this time with Anne Shelton and Sophie Tucker heading the cast, as well as the first ITV appearance of a Lancashire comic with twenty years of experience in the Music Halls, Jill Summers, who was to have her own Jack Hylton series later that year, but who is now best remembered as Phyllis Pearce in *Coronation Street*.

May ended with another new series to get viewers in the mood for summer. The idea was that the fortnightly *Hotel Riviera* would be a peek at the glamorous lives lived by those who holiday on the French Riviera. The 'hotel' was managed by French/American actor Alec D'Arcy, with Dick Bentley as a wealthy guest and Rosalina Neri as the cabaret star. The one remaining, but sadly, incomplete episode of this in the Archive's collection looks as if it is nothing more than a vehicle for Miss Neri, who has three song spots, including an operatic aria, plus a dance sequence, all within the space of a twenty-six minute programme. She also has to cope with speaking, which is unfortunate as she has a rather squeaky voice. The programme itself is obviously studio-based, and seems to have relied for its glamour on D'Arcy's French accent and Neri's Italian one.

Hylton's predilection for transferring to TV musical shows which had been stage successes continued with a production of *Waltz Time*, with Tudor Evans and Marion Grimaldi taking the leading roles. It appears to have passed by pretty well unremarked on by the press. The publicity seems to have been saved for another comedy series which was to alternate with *Hotel Riviera: Beside the Seaside* — what Philip Purser in the *Daily Mail* of 28 June 1958 called: 'A pleasing collision of winkles and champagne'. This took a rather more British look at the summer holiday, with Richard Murdoch as an entertainment manager at a seaside town and Glenn Melvyn and Danny Ross as his all-purpose assistants, Wally Binns and Alf Hall.

Summer for many people, of course, would not have been complete without a holiday visit to an end-of-the-pier show, and Hylton was able to provide just such entertainment for those folks who were staying at home when he televised excerpts from *Jump For Joy*. This was a show he was presenting with Chesney Allen at the South Parade Pier, Southsea, and which starred Reg Dixon and Sally Barnes. It's surprising that this is the only summer show which Jack Hylton televised, especially as the BBC made regular visits to end-of-the-pier shows

Sally Barnes and Reg Dixon starred in *Jump For Joy*

29

throughout the summer. It was probably simply too expensive and complicated to do any more. Hylton didn't have the facility to do outside broadcasts, and for *Jump For Joy* the scenery and cast were transported to A-R's Wembley Studio Two for the telerecording, and then conveyed back to Southsea afterwards. Jack Hylton must have liked the pairing of Dixon and Barnes, however, as later in the year he was to create a new series especially for them.

A series was also created for Jill Summers, who had gone down so well in the last *Lady Ratlings Show*. It was a change of tack for Hylton to go for a female comic, and a forty-five-year-old one too, so it must have been disappointing that the shows were considered so poor. The supporting cast for the first show included Michael Bentine and Wilfred Hyde White. Stu Knowles's comment in *Commercial Television News* of 26 July was: '*Summer's Here* uses an over-complicated formula to introduce a number of variety acts. Simplify it, prune it and tighten it — and the sun may well shine on Miss Summers'. It would seem that once again the lack of a decent script was the main hindrance to success. In the midst of all this summer jollity, Hylton chose to show an excerpt from the Crazy Gang's current London show, *These Foolish Kings*. The programme seems to have been mainly the usual slapstick humour, with the highlight being a rousing reception for the John Tiller Girls. There was also the return of *The Music Box* with a virtually all-black cast of singers and entertainers, including Hutch, Marpessa Dawn, the Limbo Boys, and the last-minute addition of Bertice Reading.

It is interesting that the *Stage* of 5 September carried a photograph and caption of an event which no other papers seemed to cover, but which is an important part of the Jack Hylton story. The picture is of Hylton and Captain Brownrigg, General Manager of Associated-Rediffusion, signing a new agreement extending 'for a considerable period' Hylton's arrangement to provide light entertainment for the company. The original agreement between Jack Hylton and A-R had been for three years, so was not due for renewal until July 1958. However, A-R was in severe financial difficulty at this time, so the financial side of their contract with Jack Hylton may well have been tightened in the new agreement. Certainly, the first contract made no mention of the sums involved, whereas the new one did. The second contract was to take effect from 13 October 1957 and would run for a period of two years, with the option of termination by either side available after that time, provided six months' notice was given. Hylton was again contracted to provide an hour of programming every fortnight and a half-hour every week. For this Jack Hylton Television Productions would be paid £3,750 for each one hour programme and £2,500 for each half-hour programme. Out of these sums the Hylton organisation was expected to pay for the script, performers, scenery and props, musical director and musicians, costumes and wigs, choreographer, rehearsal and transport costs. Associated-Rediffusion would pay for the programme director, production assistant and stage manager, make-up, hairdressing and publicity. They would also provide all the studio cameras, technical equipment, and dubbing and editing facilities when required.

For the autumn there were more new series, the first being *That's Life*, a six-part series starring Max Wall. It was possibly Hylton's most significant failure yet. Philip Purser wrote in the *Daily Mail* of 17 September: 'Max Wall launched his new ITV series last night with a show that was pretty bad even by the unexacting standards prevailing in light TV entertainment'. Once again the Jack Hylton organisation was putting out a big name in sub-standard material. Even Wall himself realised that comedy was not going to be easy on the small screen: he told the *News of the World* of 22 September 1957: 'Television is cold, impersonal for a comic. The only way you can tell if your show is good or bad is from what your employers say and from the people who buy advertising space in the show.' He would, of course, have had no idea how the show looked, as it was done live, so would have been totally dependent on others for reactions as to how it had gone.

Luckily, *Alfred Marks Time* had returned after a summer break, but it was still only going out once a month, leaving plenty of programming gaps to fill. The members of the Chinese Classical Theatre were making their first appearance in the west at the Theatre Royal, Drury Lane, and Hylton decided to devote an entire episode of *The Music Box* to the troupe. Another episode of *The Music Box* had an Irish theme, with stars from Dublin's Gaiety Theatre topping the bill.

October began with a show called *People Like Us*, the comedy series especially written for Reg Dixon and Sally Barnes after their success in *Jump For Joy*. The premise of this series was that Dixon and Barnes were residents of the 'Sunnyholme' boarding house in an ordinary provincial town. Dixon was meant to be the borough librarian, and he and shop girl Barnes were good friends, ordinary people who found themselves in funny situations as scripted by Sid Colin and Talbot Rothwell. As so often happened with Hylton comedies, what might have been gentle observational comedy gave way to farce, which led Philip Purser to write in the *News Chronicle* of 11 October 1957:

Gloomiest event of the week has been the new Reg Dixon and Sally Barnes series. Disappointment is the rule rather than the exception in television light entertainment, but it is dismaying to see the clock put back so resolutely. ... Somewhere in Hylton House comedians and writers alike lose their original and adventurous ideas. Play for the safe laugh, they are urged. "If in doubt, fall over" is the house motto.

The first episode also prompted James Thomas to write in the *Daily Express* of 8 October: 'After Max Wall, this is the second Hylton flop of the autumn shows. Tragic, because the artists are there and the ideas are there. The writers are not. Hylton, master of the theatre, does not seem able to grasp the importance of words on TV.'

At the start of the year the *Daily Express* of 19 January 1957 had a report by Thomas of an interview he had done with Hylton to ask him why he was having such trouble with his programmes, and in particular with the scripts:

> I take full responsibility for the scripts. I don't put the blame on any-one else. I have a hard time finding scripts and when I do the writers, the artists, and I often disagree on them. It's the weakest link of the lot. But I keep trying to please both a Woolworth audience and a Fortnum and Mason audience. Most people shop on the Wool-worth level.

His solution, however, was not to invest in comedy writers. Instead, he found another way of acquiring material, the results of which would be seen the following year.

The Lady Ratlings were back in October with yet another evening of feminine variety, this time with 'Two Ton' Tessie O'Shea topping the bill and apparently doing the can-can. This type of entertainment was now beginning to wear rather thin with critics (as were the Water Rats shows on the BBC), but the public was still tuning in.

In November *People Like Us* disappeared, unlamented, from the schedules after its third and final episode. By this time all pretence of being a situation comedy had gone, and the pro-gramme was mainly taken up with a variety show put on by Barnes and Dixon for their fellow boarders. This presumably meant that they could go through various old routines, abandoning any attempt at subtlety.

Another of Max Wall's *That's Life* shows, this time co-written by Johnny Speight, prompted Peter Black to comment that:

> Jack Hylton has very strong and personal ideas about what the tele-vision audience wants. He sees us — I'm deducing from what I have seen of his TV shows — as a typical Monday night audience at the Theatre Royal, Shuddersford. He knows this audience like the back

32

of his hand, and does not believe that it is any different just because it happens to number 3,000,000 or 4,000,000 instead of 26 paying customers and 54 holders of complimentary tickets; or because it is watching at home instead of in the theatre.

It is, of course, a profound misjudgement. The provincial music-hall audience is so used to making the best of its bargain that it will applaud the dimmest spark of talent or even of effort. The television audience, spoiled and capricious, has nothing in common with it, except eyes and ears.

Black seems to have hit the nail on the head here, with an astute summation of Jack Hylton's inability to thrive as a TV producer.

New for November 1957 was another series of the Arthur Askey vehicle *Before Your Very Eyes*, with the advance publicity trumpeting the fact that Askey's 'playmate' for this series would be June Whitfield, Sabrina having gone to pastures new. The first of the three programmes went out on 18 November, on the same night as the Royal Variety Performance, in which both Askey and Hylton were to appear. It seems strange, then, that although the other programmes in the series were telerecorded, the first one was moved forward an hour and done live — leaving Askey just enough time to dash from the Wembley Studios to the London Palladium. No doubt a live show gave the little man plenty of scope for ad libbing, but the other shows were recorded so that he could start rehearsals for pantomime.

November also saw *The Lady Ratlings* make their final appearance of the year with Anne Shelton leading the 'girls'. Then in December *Before Your Very Eyes* continued its run, while Alfred Marks celebrated the twentieth episode of *Alfred Marks Time*, basking in the knowledge that his was still the most critically acclaimed programme in the Jack Hylton stable, and that famous names were still happy to guest on shows.

Hylton rounded off the year with three specials, the first of which — *See You in Soho* — was billed as a look at this area of London and some of the shady characters who inhabit it. It was the usual rag-bag of musical acts, held together with the flimsiest of plots, and starring Tessie O'Shea as the owner of a coffee bar. The Christmas offering was *The Crazy Gang's Party*, a lifeless mixture of Crazy Gang business and strange guest appearances devised by Bud Flanagan. The papers had reported that viewers were to see a sketch which the Gang had performed before the Queen at the Royal Variety Performance, but this was left out because it was too long. Instead, they saw another Royal Variety Sketch, lampooning Nato, in which Flanagan, Knox and Alfred Marks repeated their stage performances, and Sir Robert Boothby MP made up the quartet.

There was quite a behind-the-scenes rumpus about this programme, with letters and memos flying between Jack Hylton, Captain Brownrigg and director Michael Westmore about who should take responsibility for the debacle. It seems that not enough studio time was allowed for the telerecording of a programme with so many scenes and guest artists, given the Crazy Gang's unavailability after 5 p.m., and recording had to go over into the next available day, two days later. In addition, because so many programmes were in preparation for Christmas, A-R didn't have the facilities for sending the rushes to the lab or for editing them once they came back, and this all had to be arranged elsewhere by the Hylton office. The resulting programme was obviously considered inadequate by all associated with it, even though it made the top ten in the ratings. It certainly seems to have had another result too, with Jack Hylton pointing out in a letter to Captain Brownrigg dated 30 December 1957:

> I may say that a very unhappy consequence of this business is that the Crazy Gang, to a man, has indicated that they do not again want to appear on commercial television with Associated-Rediffusion. I am pretty confident that some time having elapsed they will probably be persuaded to change their minds, but I am sure they will want an assurance that arrangements will be properly made for the presentation of their work, as they feel they are placing their careers in jeopardy unless the utmost care is taken by the Programme Contractor who puts them out.

Hylton was indeed able to persuade the Crazy Gang to return to the small screen but, as will be seen in the next chapter, it was a decision they would all live to regret. As for *The Crazy Gang's Party*, a brief letter from Brownrigg to Hylton on 10 February 1958 reported that it was now 'buried decently'.

The year of 1957 was seen out with a show called, appropriately, *Highlights of 1957*, although this was simply a judicious use of telerecordings from the previous two years, with Hylton and Hughie Green in a studio introducing filmed extracts of programmes like *Together Again*, *Music Box* and *The Robert Dhéry Show*. Some of the reviews also mention Shirley Bassey singing 'Burn My Candle', so Hylton must also have used the film which was shot for one of his opening variety spectaculars in 1955.

In truth, the real highlights of 1957 were probably *The Robert Dhéry Show* and *Alfred Marks Time*, both of which were a different type of humour to that normally seen on stage or TV, and which showed the value of an experienced ensemble production rather than a poorly rehearsed and scripted 'star' name. Although none of the early *Alfred*

Marks Times was recorded, the surviving Dhéry programmes have weathered the years well and are still very funny.

It was Hughie Green who helped Jack Hylton see out 1957, and Green was one of the people who would help him start 1958.

THE AMERICAN CONNECTION

Although he continued to defend his programmes, Hylton was, nonetheless, disconcerted by the critical reaction to them, and had become very anxious about the quality and range of entertainment going out under his name. It was beginning to dawn on him that you couldn't just point a camera at the stage and call it television. At the end of 1957 he had approached Hughie Green for advice on making programmes which would be entertaining and popular with both audiences and critics.

Green agreed to make programmes for Hylton, in effect as a subcontractor, provided that he was given *carte blanche* and was not simply a presenter. He had the idea that an 'interest' programme with interviews and perhaps an overall theme (an all-female show or one based on football) could be entertaining and something unique in television. Hylton handed Hughie Green complete control of these programmes, which would go out fortnightly under the title *Jack Hylton's Monday Show*.

The first of these shows was transmitted on 6 January 1958 and contained a mixture of music, dance and politics — the latter two being provided by a St Trinian's Ballet and an interview with Jennie Lee, MP. The decision to mix entertainment and politics certainly bewildered many of the critics, although Peter Black commented in the *Daily Mail* of 8 January 1958: 'I liked the idea of incorporating a short political broadcast. Light entertainment is certainly the proper context for these affairs'.

It was not, however, to the liking of Captain Brownrigg, who pointed out in a letter to Hylton dated 8 January 1958:

> In the course of this interview [Jennie Lee] managed to fire off her political opinion on the House of Lords reform ... the result was a clear breach of the Television Act for which I am apologising to the I.T.A. I must ask you in future not to include political personalities in your light entertainment half-hours since, however well intentioned they and the producer and director may be, there is always a danger that something will occur which puts the Company in a breach of Contract with the I.T.A.

On alternate weeks *Jack Hylton's Monday Show* was purely an entertainment show with comedy and music, hosted by Dick Bentley and Rosalina Neri. The two surviving programmes are very good examples of the sort of vehicle Hylton was creating for Miss Neri. Her pretensions to the world of opera were shown in the first programme, transmitted on 13 January, when she sang a duet from *La Traviata*. However, internal memos and minutes from Hylton House show that she had such a small repertoire that she would have to repeat that duet in the final programme on 7 April. In order to make it look different, the set was changed, and Neri mimed, singing to a pre-recorded tape of her own voice. Her performance on 24 March was also recorded in this way, and this was highlighted by Neville Randall in the *Daily Sketch* of 25 March. The programme of 7 April was telerecorded on 2 April, in order to fit in with Rosalina Neri's private arrangements — presumably she had arranged to be elsewhere for this Easter Monday.

Only three examples of Hughie Green's *Monday Show* have survived, two of which did so for very obvious reasons. The first of these was the novel idea of a programme recorded 30,000 feet above the Atlantic Ocean, in the hold of a BOAC Britannia airliner flying from London to New York. On board was a variety of passengers, ranging from Laurence Harvey and Donald Campbell to Winifred Atwell and Rosalina Neri. Jack Hylton himself was also on board and can be seen in the background most of the time, chomping on a fat cigar. Green had organised the whole show, and booked the aeroplane and the acts, but the original flight on 6 February had to be abandoned when the plane sprang a leak, so the performers were put up overnight in a London hotel. That night, the Munich air disaster happened, killing many of the Manchester United football team, the 'Busby Babes'; Hughie Green remembers that poor Winifred Atwell was then terrified of flying the following day.

Most of the sound for the musical acts had been pre-recorded and is now missing (indeed it appears from internal letters that the soundtrack went missing in the summer of 1958), but one performer is still there in sound and vision. She is a four-year-old child called Helen Crayford who sang and played the trumpet. Child performers under the age of twelve were not permitted to appear 'live' on television because of LCC regulations, but the law did not cover the airspace over the Atlantic, so Helen was able to perform for viewers, accompanied on the piano by Jack Hylton himself. The film was then flown back to the UK, to be ready for transmission on 17 February.

Hylton had tried to get his acts booked on American television, especially on the NBC network, while they were in New York, but without success. Meanwhile, Hughie Green had already arranged interviews with Peter Ustinov, Mary Ure and Dr Ralph Bunche, Assistant Secretary General of the UN, which were to be filmed for his next *Monday Show*. Also included was a ride on the ferry that the Queen had travelled on during her New York visit, and interviews with three British GI Brides. These items were interspersed with a number of Paddy Stone dance sequences. Unfortunately, the programme has a somewhat disjointed look, and despite its honourable intentions, it never really gels. It also suffers from terrible sound and picture quality and some very bad dubbing. Minutes of the Hylton TV committee noted that it was 'an appalling show'; Jack Hylton, who was present at the meeting, said he would write to Hughie Green to complain about it.

Jack Hylton's Monday Show was the mainstay of his programming during the first half of 1958. Alfred Marks and The Lady Ratlings continued to appear every month or so, but the accent was on light entertainment rather than comedy. Hylton continued to try the *See You in Soho* format, with scripts by Ted Willis, but as an attempt to do something different in variety it didn't really succeed, either as thriller or musical entertainment. There were two shows, in February and March, with Tessie O'Shea and Max Miller as regular faces, but the first programme was more notable for the guests who didn't appear. Buddy Holly and the Crickets had been booked for the programme on 13th March, but were later cancelled owing to a 'contractual misunderstanding'. The *Daily Mirror* of 13 March reported that Hylton alleged that the Crickets were under exclusive contract to him for ITV, and a February appearance on *Cool For Cats*, even though it was just a twenty second interview, had invalidated this. Internal Hylton memos say that the band were of insufficient quality anyway, and it may well be that Hylton had decided to cancel them because their appearance earlier in the week on *Sunday Night at the London Palladium* had not gone down too well with the critics. However, this didn't stop the BBC from featuring them in *Off The Record* on 27 March.

In April there were two more episodes of *Before Your Very Eyes*, in which Arthur Askey could be relied upon to make the most of the flimsiest of scripts. Only one show was new, however, as Askey lost his voice and was unable to take part in the second programme, so a telerecording of the live show originally transmitted on 9 March 1956 went out instead.

In May, Robert Dhéry and his company made a welcome return to British TV screens for two more episodes of *The Robert Dhéry Show*. The company had been back in France for a year, this time performing a revue called *Les Pommes a l'Anglaise*, which was based on their observations of English life. The troupe was only on British soil for a short time, so the first show, a forty-five-minute one, went out live on 8 May,

Colette Brosset, Robert Dhéry and his 'niece' in *The Robert Dhéry Show*

and the next day a thirty-minute programme was telerecorded for transmission the following fortnight.

Also in that month, a rather strange item appeared in the *Beckenham Advertiser* of 8 May about the forthcoming appearance on the BBC of Sid Caesar and Imogene Coca, the stars of the hugely popular American comedy series *Your Show of Shows*. The anonymous author begins the article by mentioning a recent appointment to take tea with Jack Hylton and Arthur Askey while watching telerecordings of some of these American shows. He then goes on to talk about the success of Caesar in the United States, and what he is likely to be doing at the BBC. A shortened copy of this article appeared in the *Liverpool Evening Express* of 29 May 1958 under the byline of Gale Pedrick.

What is strange about the article is that it does not question how Jack Hylton came to be in possession of telerecordings of *Your Show of Shows*. The author probably had no idea that Hylton had actually purchased huge quantities of scripts from Max Liebman in the USA, all of them scripts from Sid Caesar's *Your Show of Shows* from the period 1950-1954, written by people like Mel Brooks, Woody Allen and Neil Simon. Internal documents from New York theatrical agent Fred Harris to the General Manager of Jack Hylton Television Productions, Hugh Charles (also, incidentally, Hylton's brother-in-law), mention the figure of $35,000 as payment for Liebman material and a letter dated 29 October 1958 from Captain Brownrigg to Arnold (later Lord)

39

Goodman, Hylton's solicitor, refers to: 'The purchase cost of the scripts, namely, £14,000 by the Hylton organisation and £24,311 by A-R'. It seems that although Hylton had negotiated the purchase of the material, the costs were shared and Hylton was given first claim on the use of the scripts, with A-R being able to use those he didn't want.

There must have been many secret meetings within Hylton House to discuss what use could be made of the scripts. The minutes of a TV Production Committee meeting held on 22 April 1958 give some idea of the tenor of these discussions: 'It was noted that the name "Sid Caesar" should not be used in any way what so ever in the future. A decision is required as to what answer is to be given to any inquiries received about the author of these scripts — Mr Hylton to be consulted on this point.' Internal memos also give some idea of the kind of influence Hylton had before his programmes were made. He decided on titles, also on directors, and even on the acts for the variety programmes, and it is therefore likely that he decided what would be done with the Sid Caesar scripts.

Two series in 1958 made use of the sketches, the first called *On with the Show*, starring Australian actor Alan White and June Whitfield, the second *The Dickie Henderson Half-Hour*. A memo dated 1 May 1958 from Jack Hylton to Hugh Charles, Douglas Hurn, Andrew Neatrour, Bob Swash, Frank Brown, Bill Hitchcock, T. Porter and T. Hayes states: 'There must be no announcements of any kind made regarding the forthcoming Dickie Henderson and Alan White shows — i.e. regarding scripts, times of showing, etc. — without first consulting me. This is very important.'

The first appearance of the Caesar scripts was probably in *Jack Hylton's Monday Show* of 2 June 1958. This was a half-hour show with Alfred Marks and Paddie O'Neil appearing in two sketches, one of which was performed entirely in gibberish 'Italian'. These gibberish sketches had been a feature of *Your Show of Shows*, and reviewers noted that it differed from the style of comedy normally performed by Marks. Perhaps that is one of the reasons why the gibberish sketches were also to be used in the final Hylton series of *Alfred Marks Time* the following year.

The first episode of *On with the Show*, starring White and Whitfield, went out live from the Hackney Empire on 5 June 1958, and was hosted by Sidney James, with guest musical appearances by Ivor Emmanuel, Joan Manning and Kenny Baker. Press reaction seems to have been muted; the next editions on 19 June and 3 July also passed without much comment. However, news of Jack Hylton's American scripts was beginning to break in some local papers, like the *Hull Daily Mail* and *South Wales Evening Post*, where their use in *On with the Show* was noted.

The next, and perhaps most significant series to use Sid Caesar scripts was *The Dickie Henderson Half-Hour*, originally scheduled to start in mid-June, but in fact first transmitted on 4 July. As most of this series is in the NFTVA's collection, it is actually possible to compare the Henderson version of scripts with the original Caesar ones. It was a simple format: Dickie Henderson welcomed the viewers to the show, then there was a song spot from a guest singer, after which Henderson or one of his co-stars would introduce the first of (usually) two sketches. These invariably involved Dickie and Anthea Askey playing the roles of husband and rather dotty wife in various confrontational domestic situations, but may have been a spoof of a film, or a solo role for Dickie, playing an ordinary man in a restaurant or a post office queue, who can't do anything right.

The series was very popular with the public and many of the critics considered it a refreshing change from the normal light entertainment provided by ITV. Many viewers thought that Anthea and Dickie were husband and wife in real life. There was also a theatrical spin-off when Dickie and Anthea and ex-boxer Freddie Mills, who had guested on many of the programmes, toured around the country performing a 'Dickie Henderson Show'. However, the tour was rather unsuccessful

Dickie Henderson, Freddie Mills, Anthea Askey and Eve Lister in
The Dickie Henderson Half-Hour

41

as the public wanted to see a continuation of their TV roles as husband and wife, whereas what they got was versions of both Henderson's and Askey's stage acts.

It was James Green, writing in the *Star* of 8 July 1958, who broke the news about the source of Hylton's American scripts. What he didn't say was how the scripts had been adapted for a British audience, the reason being that there was no proper adaptation. Anthea Askey recollects that the cast rehearsed for three days at Hylton House, one day of which was spent watching the original Sid Caesar and Imogene Coca versions of sketches. They then went through the scripts, simply changing any words and phrases which they felt were too American.

The day after the report in the *Star*, the *Scottish Daily Express* went one further after reports that the public were finding Dickie Henderson's show much funnier than Sid Caesar's BBC series, which had begun on 1 July. James Thomas wrote:

> Reaction indicated that the audience and the people inside TV thought Henderson's material considerably better than the much-boosted Caesar's. Today I can reveal that Henderson's material had all been done years ago by Caesar in America. It was bought by Jack Hylton, who staged the Henderson show for commercial TV.

Once the big secret was out in the open there was very little comment about it, and it certainly didn't seem to harm the viewing public's appetite for *The Dickie Henderson Half-Hour*. What none of the papers knew was that Hylton had actually tried to engage Sid Caesar for a series on ITV, but although Caesar had apparently agreed, the idea had been rejected by A-R. A letter dated 31 January 1958 from Hylton to John McMillan, Controller of Programmes at A-R, states:

> In view of our very sensible decision to record everything in writing, I think it wise in a matter of this sort to record that your Company has decided that they do not wish to take advantage of the opportunity I extended to you of engaging Sid Caeser [sic] for a series of television programmes.
>
> I, personally, think the decision is unfortunate but I understand the reasons you gave me on the 'phone.
>
> He will undoubtedly make arrangements with one of the other companies and has asked me to participate which, of course, I could not have done had you wanted him.
>
> I now hope that I shall be able to participate since, apart from anything else, I think it will be very helpful in guiding me as to the best use of the script material we have bought.

Whether Hylton had anything at all to do with Caesar's BBC series is not known, but it is interesting to speculate what use he would have made of the scripts had A-R agreed to a series for Sid Caesar. Hylton's use of the Caesar scripts continued in the hour-long *On with the Show* which went out fortnightly throughout July and August, with guest comperes including Evelyn Laye and Dennis Price (and regular minor appearances by the young Barbara Windsor). *The Dickie Henderson Half-Hour* continued on a weekly basis.

When *On with the Show* finished its run, it was replaced with a series of six fortnightly programmes called *Jack Hylton Presents Alan Young*, written by and starring the Tyneside-born Canadian actor, who was later to achieve TV fame as the human partner to Mr Ed, the talking horse. In his Jack Hylton series, Young was partnered by comedienne and musical star Eleanor Drew, who had appeared in the original production of *Salad Days* and had been spotted by Hylton for his flop musical *School*. The first programme didn't make much of an impression on the critics. Writing in *Punch* on 10 September, Henry Turton commented:

> The first of his weekly half-hours ... contained two over-long sketches, each on a hackneyed theme, which should never have been offered to us without a great deal more preparation. ... I felt, too, that the use of such ad-libs as "We didn't rehearse this bit" is unforgivable. If a production is under-rehearsed we can usually tell: reminding us of the fact does not excuse it, and is not particularly funny in itself.

This series was performed live and no recordings exist to give us an idea of the sort of sketches performed, but we can perhaps get some clues from a memo in the Hylton paperwork from Bob Swash to director Douglas Hurn which states: 'The Japanese Judo expert and the 5 Cowboys are being supplied by Mickey Wood of the Mayfair Gymnasium'!

The Alan Young programmes may not have been very successful, but they were not the unmitigated disaster that the series replacing *The Dickie Henderson Half-Hour* would prove to be. As well as buying a quantity of American scripts, Hylton had also bought the UK rights to a gameshow format called *Make Me Laugh*, which had been running on ABC television in the US earlier that year. The format of the show was that members of the public had to remain straight-faced whilst various comedians tried to make them laugh. For every second they remained impassive the contestants would win a sum of money, and if they managed not to smile or laugh for the full three minutes that sum would be doubled.

Publicity for the UK version began two weeks before the first broadcast as Hylton had decided that it would be an ideal vehicle for the Crazy Gang, with Chesney Allen as Chairman. The programmes would be telerecorded, two at a time, at A-R's Wembley Studios, and contestants would be offered five shillings for every second they didn't laugh, with a top prize of £90 for those reaching the three-minute mark. There was a pretty girl — Sue Ruskin — to introduce the contestants, and each week would also see the participation of a guest celebrity, who would also try and win the same amount of money as that offered the members of the public.

The first two programmes were to be recorded on September 5, with the Crazy Gang trying desperately to raise a smile from six contestants, ranging from a bus conductor to the TV critic of the *Daily Sketch*. It was a disaster. The Crazy Gang floundered helplessly as both audience and contestants remained determinedly straight-faced. In the end they had to break the rules of the game and resort to slapstick, covering critic Leslie Watkins with flour and water. The log book kept by Senior Floor Manager, Tony Hulley, of A-R TV reports that the Jack Hylton executives present at this telerecording were so dismayed by what they saw that they decided to cancel the recording of the second programme and send the studio audience home.

It is unfortunate that there are no documents pertaining to this series in the Jack Hylton paper collection, so we will probably never know the discussions which took place about it, but it is obvious from the other five programmes in the series that extra help had to be drafted in to try and rescue it. Comedians who were to fall flat on their faces included Arthur English, Davy Kaye, Freddie Sales, Derek Roy and Al Burnett.

Watching these shows is as excruciating today as it must have been in 1958. The cancellation of the telerecording of the second show must have alerted Jack Hylton to the fact that the programme would be likely to die on its feet, and after the fifth programme Ronald Stott wrote in the *Yorkshire Evening News* of 17 October 1958:

It has made a butcher's holiday of what we commonly call 'Britain's star comedians'. Their slaughter has been wholesale, complete and without quarter. ... It has held up more professional comedians to ridicule than all the country's stage, film and television critics together could ever hope to do ... 52 solemn-as-a-judge contestants have frowned on their most valiant efforts to the tune of £1,352.

Make Me Laugh was possibly the most painful and humiliating experience of the Crazy Gang's short television life. Bud Flanagan was reported over

Richard Murdoch and Arthur Askey in *Living It Up*

a year later in the *News of the World* of 28 February 1960 as saying: 'We walked around in dark glasses for weeks after that series, we were so ashamed'; and Jimmy Nervo was quoted in the *Glasgow Weekly News*: 'We were ashamed to look the public in the face, but there was nothing we could do, because the shows were all filmed.' The Crazy Gang never again appeared on ITV under the Jack Hylton banner.

When *Make Me Laugh* finished, the Monday night slot was filled by the return of *Living It Up*, with Arthur Askey and Richard Murdoch once more ensconced in their flat at the top of Television House. Hylton had obviously been satisfied with the response to the first series, but critical reaction to its return was more muted. Indeed, although only the first show survives, newspapers reported the following week that, at the beginning of the second programme, Askey commented on the critical reaction to the first. The surviving programme is certainly a rag-bag of silly ideas and sketches with only the thinnest veneer of a storyline. Without Arthur Askey's ability to mine even the thinnest seam of humour the whole series would probably have collapsed into chaos. As it is, we can only wonder what might have resulted if Askey had been given a decent script and some original ideas. He was also busy at this time with his BBC Radio series *The Arthur Askey Show*, which was written by Bob Monkhouse and Denis Goodwin.

45

After the sixth and final Alan Young show on 6 November, Hylton filled the rest of the Thursday night slots with one-off specials. The first of these was what would turn out to be the final appearance of the Lady Ratlings, on 20 November. Peter Black, never a fan of theirs, wrote in the *Daily Mail* of 21 November 1958:

> It rarely rises above the standard offered by the kind of provincial music-hall that is now a laundry. Most of these women are married to Water Rats, and are presumably not more pressed for money than the rest of us. I imagine from the level of performance last night that most of them would be happier looking after their pubs or boarding houses, or jellying eels, or baking pies, than making spectacles of themselves on television. Yet Hylton can muster them by the score any time he likes. How? We shall probably never know.

Presumably reviews like this were just as dispiriting for the performers (people like Tessie O'Shea and Pearl Carr) as they must have been for Hylton. It was therefore farewell to the Lady Ratlings and hello to another band of old-timers, the Concert Artists' Association, for a programme called *The Entertainers* on 4 December. But not before the final appearance of Arthur Askey under the *Jack Hylton Presents* standard.

The last episode of *Living It Up* saw Arthur Askey going out with a whimper rather than a bang, which only served to underline how much this professional and well-loved performer had been ill-served by his association with Jack Hylton Television Productions. The final show was actually the episode of *Before Your Very Eyes* which had been cancelled earlier in the year owing to Askey's ill-health. This was also Askey's final series for Jack Hylton, possibly because, at a fee of £800 a show, plus the demands he made for use of certain studios, A-R felt he was proving too costly.

On paper, *The Entertainers* sounds anything but entertaining. In fact the heart sinks just reading the press previews, which promise everything from the modern music-hall bar the acrobats. Viewers were therefore served up Cyril Fletcher as compere, Elsie and Doris Waters, Flotsam, Leslie Sarony, no less than three conjurers, spoofs on *Cool For Cats* and *Oh Boy!*, and various dance routines. Three days later Hylton was able to get a good plug for a play which had transferred from Blackpool to the Victoria Palace Theatre, by showing a half-hour excerpt from it in his Thursday slot. *Friends and Neighbours*, by Austin Steele, starred the ubiquitous Glenn Melvyn and Danny Ross, with Valentine Dyall, and was the story of a Lancashire couple who invite two Russians to spend a week with them, to give the visitors a good impression of the British way of life. The play was relayed live from the Victoria Palace before a specially invited audience.

The final one-off special was a sixty-minute programme entitled *The Fastest Show on Earth*, in which twenty-two performers were given less than three minutes each to sing, dance, joke and yodel their way to fame. Most were young and relatively new to showbusiness, and virtually all were appearing, or had appeared, in summer shows and cabarets all over the country. Director Douglas Hurn devised the show and toured the venues picking out the acts who were to be given their brief moment of fame. Jack Hylton then auditioned them all and made the final selection. He also found some acts himself, including the William Deasley Quintette, of which the *Daily Sketch* of 18 December 1958 quotes Hylton as saying: 'I spotted them in The Fishmongers Arms pub at Wood Green when I nipped in for a drink'.

Whether Jack Hylton was able to keep his theatrical venues stocked with talent from this show is not recorded, but none of the names in the cast list went on to become television stars in their own right, although comedian John Comer achieved fame as Sid, owner of the café in *The Last of the Summer Wine*. Writing in the *News Chronicle* of 19 December 1958, Philip Purser was not impressed:

> The principle on which Mr Hylton based the show was presumably the old one about the moving target being harder to hit. And in a way he was right. From such a breathless parade of second-rate talents it was hard to single out the worst. Of course new performers should be encouraged. Of course TV must be always on the look out for them. But the way to nurture new people is to put a few of them into a show tailored to their particular skills. To bundle 20 together, without direction, without the slightest attempt at a unifying theme, was plain cruelty.

On 15 December, singer Anne Shelton began a series of six programmes of comedy and music for Jack Hylton, but as the first two shows were done live and not recorded, a fuller account of the series will be given in the next chapter. Anne Shelton was also Hylton's co-host in one of his last shows of the year — *Highlights of 1958*. This was actually an excuse to recycle the telerecordings of programmes presented by Jack Hylton throughout 1958. Shelton and Hylton introduced clips from *Before Your Very Eyes*, *The Dickie Henderson Half-Hour*, *The Robert Dhéry Show* and others, whilst indulging in some friendly banter. He also played the piano while Anne sang a number. It was, of course, probably easier to pay repeat fees than to create a new programme.

Hylton finally bade farewell to 1958 with a special New Year's Eve Party from the restaurant in Hylton House in Saville Row, where many of the regulars from his TV programmes were invited to do their party pieces and look as if they were having jolly good fun, while their host wandered around looking genial. Guests included Alfred Marks and Paddie O'Neil, Arthur Askey, Hughie Green, Shani Wallis and, of course, Rosalina Neri. It appears to have been a bit of a mess, with many critics mentioning its amateurishness and general muddle. One can imagine that what might have seemed like a good idea at the time was probably scuppered by the lack of rehearsal and of any overall structure. It was a fitting end to yet another indifferent year of television output from Jack Hylton Television Productions.

1959
THREE LAUGHS AND HALF A GIGGLE

There were changes afoot in 1959, the year the female stars got the big programme breaks with Jack Hylton. There would be far fewer musical variety programmes and a more determined effort to produce proper situation comedies, but this was also to be make-or-break time for Hylton's experiment with television. His contract with A-R underwent further changes, with the fortnightly hour-long programme exchanged for a weekly half-hour programme, (making two half-hours a week), at a payment to Hylton of £2,250 per half hour. Discussions about these changes had begun in the summer of 1958, with A-R's initial request being for one weekly programme of an hour's duration. Hylton was not happy with this, and in a letter dated 1 August 1958 he wrote to Captain Brownrigg: 'I know that most of the artists under contract to me (particularly the comedians) would not be prepared to do an hour's programme, and without them I would not be able to keep up the standard of programme I want to present, which would be neither good for A.R.D. or myself.' This loss of the hourly programme meant that there would be no more variety spectaculars, and a change to one of Hylton's most popular shows.

The year began with the third of Anne Shelton's programmes, a series which was now being extended from six to twelve because of its success in the ratings. She was the first woman to have such a programme on ITV, although Petula Clark, Yana and Alma Cogan had all had their own series on the BBC. She was able to have a say in the content of the shows, choosing what she would sing and sometimes suggesting the guests too. Three or four days a week were spent rehearsing the programmes at Hylton House in Saville Row, with an extra day for the music, and the programmes were then recorded at A-R's Wembley studios. Sketches were written by Dick Vosburgh and Brad Ashton, the writers of *Alfred Marks Time*. The interview spot, which was a regular feature of the programme, was done pretty much on the wing, with ideas having been discussed beforehand but no strict script. Shelton herself remembered these as being very happy shows to work on, and in particular she recalled one sketch with Michael Bentine that had to be repeated three times because one of the cameramen was laughing so much.

Anne Shelton and Edmund Purdom in *The Anne Shelton Show*

It cannot be said that the programmes were a great critical success, many of the critics commenting on the quality of the comedy spots, but Hylton was obviously pleased with them, and would have liked to have extended the series even further had Anne not already been booked for a tour of Scandinavia. *The Anne Shelton Show* was joined every week by a series called *Focus on Youth* which was hosted by Bryan Michie and purported to showcase some of the promising young talents of the day. The first programme included an interview with John Osborne and a trainee vicar who was also an escapologist. Some of those appearing, notably the Diz Disley quartet and Jeremy Lubbock, were booked to appear on further shows.

After the initial six *Anne Shelton Shows*, the programme became fortnightly for the second half of its run, alternating with a new series of *Alfred Marks Time*. This series differed from the earlier ones in a number of ways. As Marks was appearing in a play called *A Day in the Life of ...* at the Savoy Theatre, it was not going to be possible to put in the rehearsal time needed for a live one-hour programme; the change to Hylton's contract with A-R meant that there was only a thirty minute slot available anyway. The half-hour programmes were recorded at the Hackney Empire, leaving Alfred Marks just enough time to rush from Hackney to the West End to appear on stage. That was not the only change, however. Previous shows had been written by Brad Ashton and Dick Vosburgh and (uncredited) Paddie O'Neil, but for this series the ubiquitous Sid Caesar scripts were brought out of hiding again, for Vosburgh and Ashton to adapt. Not all the sketches were Caesar ones, but the use of the Caesar scripts and the change to a telerecorded half-hour format completely altered the tone of the programme — unfortunately, not for the better.

In effect, this series of *Alfred Marks Time* abandoned all the elements which had made it a critical and popular success — the decent amount of rehearsal time, properly written scripts, surprise star guests — and the end product was yet another typical Hylton half-hour. The change was immediately pounced on by TV critics, who seemed to feel that the programme itself had let them down. Philip Purser wrote in the *News Chronicle* of 3 February 1959: 'The old *Alfred Marks Time* was a pioneer in the business of poking robust fun at other departments of tele-vision ... A new formula was clearly desirable. But cutting the old one in two and throwing the better half away was hardly the way to do it.'

The general feeling was that the programme had suddenly gone horribly wrong, and it had lost the sense of fun and freshness that had always kept it head and shoulders above all the other Jack Hylton out-put. The second in the series fared even worse. Special guest Spike Milligan was so busy with writing and recording *The Goon Show* for the BBC, that his appearance as a visiting German General had to be severely cut because he couldn't spare the time to attend rehearsals, and he was filmed on the empty Hackney Empire stage. In addition, because there had been lighting difficulties the programme had been telerecorded with temporary lighting which proved to be inadequate for the picture quality. As a result, the transmission was cancelled at the last minute and the show had to be replaced with a short film called *It Shouldn't Happen to a Dog*. The cancelled programme was transmitted on 30 March instead, and Hylton managed to get A-R to agree it as an extra programme outside his contract, thus receiving an additional payment for it. It is unfortunate that the only episodes of *Alfred Marks Time* in the NFTVA's collection are the five episodes of this very disap-pointing series: the jewel in Jack Hylton's crown survives only as paste.

Alfred Marks Time and *The Anne Shelton Show* continued on alter-nate Mondays, and *Focus on Youth* drew to a close on 18 February with a song from Shirley Bassey and an interview with Tommy Steele's manager. It was replaced by the Italian singer Rosalina Neri, who was finally given her very own series. Rosalina had been guesting on Hylton shows since 1956, and various methods of presenting her had been tried, but her new series, called simply *The Rosalina Neri Show*, was a mixture of solos and duets for Rosa and her co-star, Welsh tenor Ivor

Emmanuel. There were no comedy sketches, so no scriptwriters were necessary, and there was a guest artist each week. This was also the first Jack Hylton series to be directed by the distinguished Milo Lewis, famous at that time for directing *The Army Game*. He had resigned from Granada TV in order to join the Hylton organisation.

Rosalina actually made the cover of the *TV Times* for the 22-28 February edition, and there was plenty of publicity surrounding her launch as a fully-fledged TV star. According to publicity handouts, she had just returned from making a film in Italy, and would be returning there for some TV appearances before the series was through. The first four in the series were probably done live, but the last two were telerecorded.

Neri was promoted heavily as a sexy Latin lovely. Certainly her figure had rather more obvious appeal than her voice, as the two telerecorded programmes show. She often appeared in press cuttings which emphasised her vital statistics and womanly charms, but even in the unliberated 1950s her lack of singing ability did not go unquestioned by many of the nation's TV critics. Comments ranged from: 'still without a voice to match her vital statistics' (*Liverpool Echo*, 12 March 1959) to: 'Rosalina Neri, the Italian blonde bombshell, has a glorious figure, but she is a shockingly bad singer' (Ken Hatzer, *Manchester Evening Chronicle*, 12 April 1959). Rosalina sang mainly in Italian and French, probably because her English was still very poor and she had a very strong Italian accent. Indeed, the surviving programmes demonstrate that when she did occasionally sing in English it proved to be almost impossible to understand what she was saying. In the final programme in the series she even started 'la la la-ing' and admitted that she had forgotten the words. It would seem that 1959 was rapidly turning into a bit of a disaster for Jack Hylton TV Productions, but there was considerably worse publicity still to come.

The Rosalina Neri Show came to an end on 2 April, and was replaced on 9 April by the first of a six-part series starring Cyril Fletcher. This was a sketch series called *The Cyril Fletcher Show*, written by Johnny Speight and starring Fletcher, his wife, Betty Astell, and Pat Coombs. Only the first programme survives, and it is a fascinating example of what the Jack Hylton organisation was doing with its comedy series. The telerecording in the NFTVA has two separate soundtracks, one with all the dialogue from the sketches and the odd laugh here and there, and the other with all the dialogue plus raucous canned laughter which often covers the punchlines. In working out which was the soundtrack used for transmission one only had to look at the reviews. Philip Purser asked in the *News Chronicle* of 10 April 1959: 'Where do they find that maniacal studio audience?' and a report in the *Wolverhampton Express & Star* of 10 April said:

'The obviously dubbed cackles of an unseen audience [were] more than flesh and blood could stand. Often it seemed that the laughter came in the wrong places. I say "seemed" because it was by no means easy to detect which would have been the right places.' It is likely that the programme was recorded in front of a studio audience but that the lack of audience laughter — owing, no doubt, to the unfunny material — meant that an alternative soundtrack had to be made, with canned laughter very inexpertly added. If press cuttings are anything to go by, it is safe to assume that the series didn't improve.

There was another intriguing aspect to this series, however, which got some coverage in the press. A news item in the *Sunday Pictorial* of 3 May 1959 remarked on the fact that Jack Hylton was going to show some film of Shirley Bassey and David Hughes in *The Cyril Fletcher Show*. This did not go down well with Bassey and Hughes, both of whom felt that their careers had taken off in different directions since the film had been recorded. Indeed, Bassey had started the year with her first number one record: 'As I Love You'. She offered to record new songs especially for the programme, and this was picked up on 7 May in the *Daily Herald*, with Philip Phillips reporting:

Coloured singer Shirley Bassey and tenor David Hughes tried to stop a TV show last night. They appealed to Jack Hylton not to screen a four-year-old film on them in tonight's *Cyril Fletcher Show*. Both singers claim their styles and features have changed in four years. ... [Shirley Bassey's] agent, Mr Peter Charlesworth said: "Millions of viewers will believe they are watching Shirley 'live'. Her face, her hairstyle, the way she sings, all these have changed. I appealed to the Hylton Organisation not to show them. We were rebuffed."

It is fairly safe to assume that Hylton had intended to use the four-year-old film excerpts shot for his opening *Jack Hylton Presents* programmes in September 1955, since the 'guest appearance' by Jack Tripp in the first *Cyril Fletcher Show* is from the same stable. Other guest artists mentioned in newspapers, such as the Tiller Girls, suggest that the Hylton archive of 1955 was raided quite considerably for this series.

Both *The Anne Shelton Show* and *Alfred Marks Time* reached the end of their runs during April, and with the latter in particular, the critics were not sorry to see it go — it had become a shadow of its former self. They were replaced by a second series of *The Dickie Henderson Half-Hour* and the return of *Focus on Youth*.

This time, there was a credit on the Dickie Henderson programmes for 'Script Associate: Jimmy Grafton', which indicates that the method of anglicising the scripts was rather more formal by now, but in every other respect the series was the same. All the programmes were telerecorded as Henderson was due to appear on stage in Blackpool over the summer. The opening song was now sung by Henderson himself, but there was still a song spot in the second half of the programme; in the one transmitted on 18 May the guest singer was Renate Holm, who had made her British TV debut three months previously in the first series of *Focus on Youth*. Dickie and Anthea were also honoured with a comic-strip version of their adventures on the front cover of *TV Fun* comic, available every Monday priced 4d.

The new series of *Focus on Youth* featured, among many now-forgotten names, twenty-seven-year-old Anthony Newley, and Ted Braithwaite, author of *To Sir With Love*, neither of whom could really have been described as youthful. The other programmes in the series contained the usual strange mixture of people: black singers and student jazz bands; a curvy Italian singer who wasn't Rosalina Neri; the contestants from the Miss Soho beauty pageant; and Greville Janner (prior to his becoming an MP) and the Brady Ramblers singing Hebrew folk songs. 'We were absolutely thrilled to appear with Jack Hylton and an array of real stars', remembers Janner.

Dickie Henderson continued his run of telerecorded programmes until the end of June, when his replacement was to be a great favourite of the time, Eric Barker, in a new sitcom called *Something in the City*. This was something of a departure for Hylton, in as much as it took the form of a proper situation comedy. Previous Hylton sitcoms had made great play of starting out with a complete storyline each week, but, whether it was *Living It Up* or *People Like Us*, they had very quickly degenerated into a series of unconnected sketches and variety turns.

Eric Barker was a very popular performer, who had up until that time written and appeared in comedy shows on BBC radio and television. For Jack Hylton he was going to appear with his wife, Pearl Hackney, in a series which was not self-penned, but had a very well-hidden pedigree. There is no hint on the telerecordings, and nothing in the TV Times or the Jack Hylton paperwork, to suggest who wrote *Something in the City*, but its origins can be traced, yet again, to Sid Caesar. In the successor to *Your Show of Shows — Caesar's Hour —* the most popular recurring sketch was one called 'The Commuters', which was sometimes extended to fill the whole hour. The sketches concerned the lives of suburb-dwellers who take the same train into the city every morning and return on the same train every night. Hylton must have bought these scripts together with all the other Sid Caesar material he purchased. Eric Barker was probably not first choice to enact them for a British audience. Indeed, an internal Jack Hylton Television

Productions memo from Bob Swash to Hugh Charles, dated 11 November 1958, indicates that actors initially considered for the roles included Daniel Massey, Bernard Cribbins, Gerald Harper, Eric Thompson, Michael Bryant, Des O'Connor, Henry McGee, Millicent Martin and Barbara Windsor.

How Hylton persuaded Eric Barker to take on the role of George Keyes is not recorded — perhaps it was the fact that it was his first regular TV series in four years — Barker is also quoted in press cuttings as saying that it was nice not to have to write a script as well as perform. There is no indication of who anglicised the scripts, but it's highly probable that Barker did this himself. *Something in the City* starred Deryck Guyler and Joan Benham as well as Eric Barker and Pearl Hackney, as two mature suburban couples, with Peter Hammond and Diane Hart as a younger one.

Some of the episodes have a clear story, others are obviously just two sketches, one on either side of the commercial break, with a very tenuous link made between them. The first in the series was transmitted on 6 July 1959, and resulted in the following review from Peter Black in the *Daily Mail* of 7 July:

> With pain and sorrow I watched Eric Barker making his television debut under the Jack Hylton banner. Gone was the wit that used to spring from Barker's personal view of life. Gone was the sense of pace and style. There remained the gormless chump convention, the genteel, southern-county-by-pass-suburban idiom which gets its laughs from making the comedian seem a bigger simpleton than anyone watching him. I never thought Barker could be persuaded to play ducks and drakes so easily with his hard-won reputation.

The situations that occupy the three couples in this series are much like those in *The Dickie Henderson Half-Hour*, where the comedy is based on confrontation and misunderstanding, usually between the sexes. It seems to have been a particular feature of the Sid Caesar material, whether used by Dickie Henderson or Eric Barker. Hylton seemed to have a knack of persuading established stars to throw away their reputations by appearing in programmes with unsuitable and poor quality material.

Eric Barker was not the only comedian who had created a successful comic career using self-penned scripts but who fell from grace by using someone else's for Jack Hylton. The series which replaced his, suffered the same fate. *Focus on Youth* and *Something in the City* ended at the end of July/beginning of August, and were replaced by *All For Pleasure* and *Gert and Daisy*. *All For Pleasure*, which began a run of six programmes on August 4, had been given the working title *Other*

People's Jobs. The idea was to build a variety show around a different job every week, the first one being hairdressing. The viewers were therefore treated to an interview with Mr 'Teazie Weazie' Raymond; Sir Donald Wolfit performing an excerpt from *Sweeney Todd, the Demon Barber*; Billy Russell singing 'Get Your Hair Cut'; and Ivor Emmanuel singing 'Jeanie with the Light Brown Hair'. This was not a series which went down well with the critics, in fact Jack Hylton's productions were now beginning to receive what were probably his worst ever reviews, and they came thick and fast for Eric Barker's replacement: *Gert and Daisy.*

Publicity for this series said that writer Ted Willis had got the idea for a TV sitcom starring Elsie and Doris Waters whilst watching them in a commercial break. Their brother, Jack Warner, had become a TV star in a drama series created by Ted Willis — *Dixon of Dock Green* — so perhaps Willis was assumed to have a lucky touch. He was also on the board of Jack Hylton Television Productions. The Waters sisters had years of experience working the music halls, and as 'Gert' and 'Daisy', had written themselves two very popular characters and a successful radio series. However, like Eric Barker, they made the mistake of appearing with scripts which they had not written themselves.

The basic premise of the series was that Gert and Daisy were soft-hearted landladies, running theatrical digs for an assortment of small-time variety performers. Gert and Daisy would open the programme by chatting to the viewers and inviting them into the boarding-house, where there was bound to be some sort of comic situation developing. Sadly, the comic situations were old and tired and stretched out far too long. Because the scripts were written by a variety of writers the characterisations of Gert and Daisy were not allowed to develop, and the result was something of a disaster. The first episode received a virtually unanimous critical mauling. Norman Hare wrote in the *News Chronicle* of 11 August: 'Jack Hylton, Ted Willis and Elsie and Doris Waters added up to about three laughs and half a giggle, in a situation comedy that smelt of moth balls'. Peter Black commented in the *Daily Mail* of the same date:

> Elsie and Doris Waters last night became the latest in a long line of favourites to submit themselves to the Hylton treatment. If they came off no worse than the Crazy Gang, Arthur Askey and Eric Barker, they came off no better. ... Last night's script, showing Gert and Daisy in a theatrical boarding-house, was indistinguishable from any film script written in the early 1930s at so much a yard by writers who would have starved if the quota regulations had not created work for them ... The dear old things did their best. The idea

56

that any alteration of their technique could be necessary for television had not occurred to them, but as it had not occurred to anybody else one cannot reproach them too bitterly.

Even the affection felt by many of the TV critics for the Waters sisters couldn't alter the fact that *Gert and Daisy* was barely passable as entertainment. The other five episodes, although not written by Ted Willis, served up the same sort of tired situations as the first. Any attempt to broaden the comedy by concentrating on some of the other boarders failed miserably because the characters were mere ciphers. The chirpy banter which had been a feature of Gert and Daisy's variety and radio act was also lost with the necessity to try and follow a plot involving other characters every week. Philip Phillips in the *Daily Herald* of 24 August wrote:

> Gert and Daisy — Elsie and Doris Waters — are angry. Their first-ever TV series has been given the thumbs down by the critics ... Doris said: "We don't think it is too bad. A lot of viewers have said they like it. What do you think is wrong?" I replied: "It lacks the wit of your radio shows, and the situations are trite." ... Then she revealed: "We write all our radio scripts."

Once again a Jack Hylton TV series was sinking like a lead weight. Even a cursory viewing of the series reveals that it lurched from banality to rudimentary farce, via the death of variety. The third episode is probably the saddest of all, with Gert and Daisy trying to find bookings for two of their lodgers when it is obvious, even to these two ladies, that the old troupers concerned are past it. Like Eric Barker, Elsie and Doris Waters found that working for Jack Hylton with someone else's scripts was detrimental to their reputation.

Someone who was kept very busy with Jack Hylton programmes was Ivor Emmanuel. *All For Pleasure* continued for a run of six episodes, each one taking a different profession as its theme, but none of them finding much favour with the critics. Although Emmanuel himself was always favourably received, the main area of complaint was that the programmes had been thrown together, inadequately rehearsed, and were very poorly scripted. An article by Kenneth Baily in the *People* of 30 August 1959 summed up much of the criticism being levelled at Hylton:

> *All For Pleasure* is regularly spoiling good acts by wrapping them up with corny gags, tatty dancers and boy-scout-hut sets, slung on at bargain prices. ... Why, oh why, does Jack Hylton go on spoiling talent for a ha'porth of material ... to Jack Hylton, whose pre-TV

The Rosalina Neri Show was a showcase for the Italian singer

achievements I shall always admire, I just say: Why become the most criticised show provider on TV at the end of such a glorious show-business career?

All For Pleasure and *Gert and Daisy* finished their runs in mid-August. They were replaced by a second series of *The Rosalina Neri Show* and another Ted Willis-devised sitcom: *Tell it to the Marines*. Rosalina was once again partnered by Ivor Emmanuel and the format was virtually the same as in her earlier series. Poor Rosalina — with the best will in the world she was never going to make it as a singer. This time she sang many more songs in English, although she was still very difficult to understand; only two of the programmes bothered with guest artists. Some of the programmes were recorded on the new two-inch videotape which was just starting to be used by the television industry.

Tell it to the Marines was Jack Hylton's attempt to emulate the success of Granada TV's hugely popular situation comedy *The Army Game*, which had made stars of many of its cast and given the nation a number of new catch phrases. Hylton's series was based around the 'friendly' rivalry between the Navy and the Marines, and although Willis devised it, scripts were written by other writers, including Malcolm A. Hulke and Eric Paice of *Gert and Daisy*, and Brad Ashton and Dick Vosburgh of *Alfred Marks Time* and *The Anne Shelton Show*. Some of the stars became familiar faces, like Ronald Hines and Henry McGee, and the director was the former director of *The Army Game*, Milo Lewis.

The first episode was received no better in most quarters than the comedy series it had replaced. The *Stage and Television Today* reviewed it as: 'A ghastly mess. A comedy show devoid of comedy, devoid of story, devoid of wit', while Peter Black reported in his *Daily Mail* 'Teleview' of 1 October: 'Once again the episode of Jack Hylton's *Tell it to the Marines* was not the episode billed in the *TV Times*. I get the impression that someone is frantically shuffling the pack of recordings, trying to find an edition that is worth showing. This is a forlorn quest if ever there was one.' Unfortunately for posterity, although the series had been recorded on videotape at the time, the tapes were all wiped by A-R, much against Hylton's wishes and intention.

By now the complaints in the press about the quality of the programmes going out under the Jack Hylton Presents banner were so many, and so deadly, that A-R obviously decided that enough was enough. Hylton had always pointed to the viewing figures whenever he was admonished about the quality of his fare, but that excuse was now wearing thin. However, his only public rebuke at this time was from the ITA, which reprimanded him for appearing in a Labour Party Political Broadcast even though his position as a main shareholder and director of TWW prevented him from any expression of political opinion. Behind the scenes, however, important decisions had been made about Jack Hylton's future as a television producer.

Not all the negotiations between Jack Hylton and A-R were recorded, but it is obvious that the relationship between the two companies was changing, and Hylton decided that the changes were not to his advantage. On 23 September 1959 he sent the following letter to Captain Brownrigg, General Manager of A-R:

I have been thinking over our conversation the other day, and I am afraid that, despite your flattering suggestion that our association should continue, I cannot see any realistic basis on which this is possible. Accordingly, I have decided that I do not want to continue with any arrangement which binds my freedom of action, or, as I am afraid has rather happened in the past, prevents me from expressing my own individuality as I have always done in the theatre. I am satisfied that my interests are better served by keeping myself free of this kind of commitment. Therefore, would you regard this letter as my formal notice to terminate our agreement on April 13th, 1960.

59

The following statement was issued to the press from Hylton House about 17 November: 'Jack Hylton wishes to announce that he has given notice to Associated-Rediffusion to terminate his contract with them as a programme contractor next April. His plans for the future are complete and an announcement about them will be made at an appropriate time.' The news was widely reported in the press on 18 November, and a very interesting article by Romney Sutton appeared in *Stage and Television Today* on 26 November 1959 in which he asked some very pertinent questions about the split between Hylton and A-R:

> What has brought this about? Bad shows? Bad press? Bad relations? It could be any of those things. It's probably all of them. .... [Jack Hylton] formed his own production company and signed an agreement with A-R to provide them with a number of shows each year under the Hylton Banner ... Under the arrangement with Associated-Rediffusion he was wholly responsible for his Light Entertainment and A-R had little, if anything, to say in the matter ... It has been known for a long time that A-R were unhappy about their set-up with Hylton, and to an extent the Press has been one of the main instruments in bringing about the final parting.

In the *Daily Mail* of 18 November Douglas Marlborough reported: '[Jack Hylton] said last night: "A-R haven't dropped me. I told them two months ago by letter that I didn't want to carry on when our contract ends next April. I have other plans for TV. I'll issue a statement when I feel it's ready."'

Many of the reports estimated that Hylton's contract with A-R had been for £100,000 a year. Also reported was the fact that Hylton himself received a consultancy fee of £30,000 a year. James Thomas in the *Daily Express* of 18 November went slightly further, reporting that: 'for some time Hylton has been discussing his future in television with programme chiefs of Associated-Rediffusion. Senior producers of Associated-Rediffusion have been pressing the company to run its own variety shows, independent of the Hylton organisation.' This is a particularly interesting detail as it points to the fact that pressure to terminate Hylton's contract came not just from A-R executives but also from the members of the company's production staff, who obviously felt they could make much better programmes than those provided by Hylton.

Hylton was keeping quiet about his future plans, but many of the papers also reported later that month that Mrs Topham, Managing Director of Aintree racecourse, was having discussions with the BBC about the televising of The Grand National of 1960, though she had also received an offer from Jack Hylton to televise it for ITV. Hylton, who was a great horseracing fan, had obviously stepped in quite late in the negotiations with a rival offer. The *Manchester Evening Chronicle* of 28 November 1959 reported: 'One of Mr Hylton's executives said today: "Jack has kept this one to himself. It is one of his own ideas and he has not said anything about it"'. In the end, of course, the BBC won the contract and James Thomas reported in the *Daily Express* of 9 December: 'Impresario Jack Hylton, who bid for the rights on behalf of commercial TV, was left at the post. Mrs Topham said: "He rang up and offered to negotiate but I gave him, as a guide, the figure we expected to get in cash from the newsreels. I never heard from him again."'

There was one more series, which had been announced some weeks in advance, and which was an attempt to add a touch of culture to the normal variety fare offered by Hylton. He signed an agreement with the Sadlers Wells Opera company to present potted versions of famous operettas in a series called *Gay Operetta*. This involved boiling down the operetta to approximately twenty-five minutes, fitting in all the well-known music and songs, and having a narrator to explain the plot. Dudley Glass was the man responsible for adapting all six operettas. The three examples of this series which survive — *The Merry Widow*, *The Gipsy Baron* and *Countess Maritza* — prove just how difficult it is to fit a quart into a pint pot. Like the second Rosalina Neri series, *Gay Operetta* was also recorded on the newly available two-inch videotape. When one considers that the cost of a tape in 1959 was the equivalent of £1,500 today, it is obvious that Hylton had invested a considerable amount of money in videorecording these two series. The three programmes in the NFTVA are also the last of Jack Hylton's television output which are known still to exist.

Gay Operetta was accorded a double page spread in the *TV Times* for its launch. The Sadlers Wells company (which would later become English National Opera) had been performing operettas at the London Coliseum, the largest theatre in London, and the change to a small TV studio severely cramped what the company was able to do. Hylton himself was not happy that so little time was available for such a prestigious company and tried to get A-R to allow a longer slot, but they were adamant that the ITV network wouldn't allow it. James Thomas reported in the *Daily Express* of 31st October: 'I have never ended up so thoroughly exhausted in my life after half an hour'.

After this attempt at culture, Hylton obviously decided to cut his losses and not bother with anything new. With his contract finishing on April 13 1960 there was little incentive to provide viewers with new or potentially long-running programmes. The year 1959 closed with the continuing adventures of *Tell it to the Marines* and he made good use of the fact that *The Dickie Henderson Half-Hour* was telerecorded by starting a repeat run of eight episodes of the second series, the most which Equity would allow him to repeat. Philip Phillips reported in the *Daily Herald* of 26 November:

> The news surprised A-R chiefs yesterday. A spokesman for Mr Hylton said last night: "All but two of the 18 [*Dickie Henderson Half-Hours*] were in the Top Ten programmes. Now, because we have received so many demands from viewers, Mr Hylton has decided to choose eight of the best shows and screen them again".

Hylton had also been influenced by the fact that the BBC had repeated seven *Hancock's Half-Hour* programmes and seven of Charlie Drake's series *Drake's Progress*, and the ratings had been higher second time around for both of them.

It had been make-or-break year for Jack Hylton Television Productions, and many more well-known names had cause to regret their association with the 'Jack Hylton Presents' flag. Dickie Henderson and Anthea Askey had been been fairly successful, but Elsie and Doris Waters, Eric Barker and Cyril Fletcher had all jeopardised their careers by appearing in shoddy programmes; Anne Shelton had done her career no harm, but had proved she was no comedian; Alfred Marks had dropped a winning formula and been found wanting. There was really nowhere for Hylton to go in 1960.

THE FINAL CURTAIN

With Jack Hylton's career as a TV producer finishing four months into the year, there was no incentive for him to produce exciting new programmes. His original ambition of bringing the best of variety into the home had long since fallen foul of his inability to translate his stage successes onto the small screen. The year began with a re-run of *The Dickie Henderson Half Hour* originally transmitted on 1 June 1959. January continued with Dickie Henderson and *Tell it to the Marines*, which was still being panned by the critics but started the year with its sixteenth episode. These two programmes ran throughout the whole of January, and *Tell it to the Marines* continued into February. The Henderson repeats were replaced in February by *Life Begins at Eighty*, which was described thus in the press release:

> It will feature the problems of octogenarians. There will be a panel of 'over-eighties' who will answer questions in viewers' letters and recall interesting incidents from their own lives. Two guineas will be paid for any viewer's letter used in the programme. ... It is also planned to include an 80-year-old celebrity in the programme each week.

Life Begins at Eighty was not new, it had already been going out as a local programme in the TWW area. It would therefore have required very little extra effort to make it a networked series. It was hosted by the ubiquitous Bryan Michie, and the discussion panel was headed by an eighty-seven-year-old cigar-smoking actress called Ada Reeve — and she was the youngest on it! In the *News Chronicle* of 6 February 1960, Philip Purser wrote of it: 'Like a hard-pressed general sending his last old depot pensioners into the line, Jack Hylton last night mobilised *Life Begins at Eighty* for the ITV network. What was originally a modest regional item in the West Country became a national threat.'

Researchers for the series raided Darby and Joan Clubs and old folk's homes around the country to try and find octogenarians able to take part in the programme. There are very few major reviews of the programme — most of the press cuttings are from local newspapers, reporting the appearance of local pensioners. One can imagine, however, that the series was much more suited to the previous local format than as prime-time networked entertainment. It was scheduled for seven o'clock on Friday nights, in between *Life with the Lyons* and *Emergency – Ward 10*.

Life Begins at Eighty lasted for eight episodes, the final one being transmitted on 25 March 1960. It was replaced by a two-part series called *The Music Goes Round*, starring singer Ronnie Hilton. Joan Savage and Adelaide Hall were among the guests in the first programme, and Carole Carr and Elaine Delmar among those in the second. Hylton had been trying to do a series with Ronnie Hilton for some time, so perhaps these two programmes were easy to produce as a swan song. The final appearance of the 'Jack Hylton Presents' logo on the ITV network came on 13 April 1960, with the thirtieth and final episode of the universally reviled *Tell it to the Marines*.

EPILOGUE

With the benefit of hindsight, it is easy to see why Jack Hylton failed to set the small screen alight during his time as an independent TV producer. The late 50s were a time of prodigious change on British television screens. Today's viewers are so used to having at least four channels to choose from that the days of one BBC channel only are a dim and distant memory. The coming of commercial television was an exciting breath of fresh air, bringing all sorts of new fare for viewers: from quiz shows like *Take Your Pick*, American cowboy series like *Wagon Train* and bold new current affairs programmes like *This Week*. Many of these programmes are still fondly remembered today, of course, even if they wouldn't pass muster with a sophisticated modern audience. Jack Hylton had the chance to produce programmes starring some of the most popular stars of the variety stage, programmes which could have become ensconced in the national consciousness in much the same way as *Sunday Night at the London Palladium* or *Double Your Money*, yet practically every programme he made has been consigned to oblivion. Even when people remember series like *The Dickie Henderson Half-Hour*, they tend to think of the 60s version, co-starring June Laverick, rather than Hylton's.

The most obvious problem with the programmes which went out under the 'Jack Hylton Presents' flag is that it took Hylton a long time to accept the fact that what was successful on a theatre stage wasn't automatically successful on a television screen. The earliest programmes were straight films of variety or stage shows, with cheaper slots using 'ordinary' people. Hylton had to balance the books by alternating the top-line entertainers he had promised A-R with cheaper programmes. The filming of stage shows also meant that Hylton didn't have to bother with new sets and scenery, which kept his costs down.

Artists under contract to Hylton's stage shows were employed for his programmes, and attempts to find new stars consisted of thrusting people who had been moderately successful in a local variety theatre or summer show straight into badly-written and ill-conceived series. These were the days when you really could be 'spotted' and given a slot on national television, but established stars who found themselves working for Jack Hylton soon discovered that reputations could be severely damaged as well as created by television.

Above all, there seems to have been a lack of imagination on the part of the Hylton organisation, an inability to think of new and exciting ideas for light entertainment. Instead of relying on Hylton's considerable theatrical contacts and expertise, the company should really have been thinking purely in televisual terms. On the odd occasion when this happened the results were encouraging, such as *Alfred Marks Time*, but all too often, attempts to re-create the atmosphere of a club or stage review simply didn't work.

In many respects Hylton's programmes were part of an 'old boy network': surely no other company would have televised the Lady Ratlings, or tried to fit the anarchy of the Crazy Gang into the living room. What the Hylton collection shows, however, is precisely the sort of entertainment that was being served up to London and provincial theatre audiences. It is also a record of the stage acts of some legendary names in variety theatre. Comedians and dancers much like the ones seen in a programme like *Jump For Joy* were appearing in seaside towns the length and breadth of Great Britain. Although the BBC televised many summer variety shows, from George and Alfred Black's Blackpool shows at the Palace Theatre to *Pleasure Boat*, a variety show presented from a different pleasure boat each week, none was recorded, so *Jump For Joy* is possibly the only example in existence.

The Crazy Gang are still talked about with great affection by people who saw their stage shows. The telerecording of their Victoria Palace revue *Jokers Wild* is possibly the only film of the Gang actually performing their routines before a live theatre audience and is therefore the only way a contemporary audience can come close to understanding what made them so popular. *The Robert Dhéry Show* captured a new and cultish type of humour which was a sensation in its time, and *Together Again* is an incomparable record of the sketches and songs with which Bud Flanagan and Chesney Allen made their names.

The collection is also, of course, an indication of the sort of programmes which the public were watching and (presumably) enjoying in the late 1950s. We are fortunate that so many excellent TV reviews were written at that time, allowing us a more critical view of the way Jack Hylton's TV programmes compared to the other offerings set before the viewers. Although it is fair to say that someone like James Thomas was encouraged to write critical reviews because Express newspapers were rivals to Associated Newspapers, part owners of A-R, Peter Black was allowed to write completely independent reviews for the Associated Newspaper-owned *Daily Mail*. Indeed, as Black had previously been a theatre critic, he was well aware of the quality of show being performed in provincial variety theatres and how Jack Hylton's programmes measured up. When one considers how easy it is for modern critics, with preview copies of programmes available on video, the fact that critics like Black, Thomas and Philip Purser had to write their reviews more or less as they watched the programmes, before phoning them in to their newspapers, makes the quality of their writing all the more impressive.

Very little of the television output from the late 50s exists — especially light entertainment, a genre often considered lightweight and unimportant — and we are very lucky that such a fascinating collection as the Jack Hylton one has survived, allowing modern audiences to savour the light entertainment programmes which were a staple diet of viewers of the nascent commerical television network.

THE JACK HYLTON COLLECTION

Over one hundred of the programmes produced by Jack Hylton for Associated-Rediffusion have survived, from early Crazy Gang shows to Eric Barker's sitcom. The following pages list all those viewed by the author, in alphabetical order, and give brief details of each series, plus episode contents and credits. Also included are additional critical comments and points of interest gleaned from the Hylton files.

ALFRED MARKS TIME

Originally a highly successful monthly programme of one hour in length. By 1959 Hylton's contractual obligations had changed and he had lost the hour slot. Alfred Marks had theatre commitments, so the programme was moved to the Hackney Empire, changed to a telerecorded half-hour, and used up some of the Sid Caesar sketches bought by Jack Hylton which were then re-written by Vosburgh and Ashton. It was not a success. Some of the opening sequences are incomplete.

(TX 2.2.59)
Sketches are: a butler and maid arguing with each other whilst serving guests; a spoof film trailer for 'Private Wives'; 'Der Prinz und Der Poppa' a spoof of *The Student Prince* performed in cod-German. Ray Ellington sings 'There Will Never Be Another You', Paddie O'Neil and Ray Ellington sing 'There's Going To Be a Great Day'.

Credits
Appearing with Alfred Marks were Paddie O'Neil, Jimmy Hanley, Leslie Mitchell, Glen Mason, Anita West, Michael Segal, John Abineri, Ex-RSM Brittain.

The Ray Ellington Quartet; Steve Race and His Orchestra; Orchestrations by Frank Davis; Scripts by Jack Hylton Scripts Ltd and Dick Vosburgh and Brad Ashton; Settings by Bernard Carey; Directed by Douglas Hurn.

Alfred Marks is now appearing in *A Day in the Life of...* at the Savoy Theatre.

Notes
Philip Purser wrote in the *News Chronicle* of 3 February 1959: 'In his darkest days as a provider of TV entertainment, Jack Hylton always had the consolation of

Alfred Marks Time once a month. Now even that old stalwart has taken a turn for the worse, judging by its return last night in a new, shorter form.' Earlier in the evening Glen Mason had appeared on the BBC singing a possible Eurovision entry.

(TX 2.3.59)
Brittain introduces the show by shouting 'Alfred Marks Time'. The first sketch is 'La Grand Amour', performed in cod French, the second is a spoof of *A Star Is Born*. Ray Ellington and Paddie O'Neil sing 'That Old Black Magic'.

Credits
Appearing with Alfred Marks were Paddie O'Neil, Patrick Barr, Paul Carpenter, Leslie Mitchell, Kent Walton, Deirdre Sullivan, Anita West, John Abineri, Ex-RSM Brittain, Roger Winton, Geoffrey Wright, Leonard Webb.

The Ray Ellington Quartet; Steve Race and his Orchestra; Orchestrations by Alan Braden; Scripts by Jack Hylton Scripts, Dick Vosburgh and Brad Ashton; Settings by Bernard Carey; Directed by Douglas Hurn.

Alfred Marks is now appearing in *A Day in the Life of...* at the Savoy Theatre.

Notes
The sketch in part two was deliberately not given a spoof *A Star Is Born* title because Vosburgh and Ashton had just been sued by Rodgers and Hammerstein for sending up *The King And I*. The BBC transmitted *A Day in the Life of...* on 5 March 1959.

(TX 16.3.59)
The first sketch is called 'Dinner For Two', the second is 'Twelve Little Words', a spoof of *Three Little Words*. Ray Ellington sings 'Got My Girl' and 'Too Marvellous For Words'.

Credits
Appearing with Alfred Marks were Paddie O'Neil, William Sylvester, Miriam Karlin, Leslie Mitchell, Jeremy Hawk, Robert Rietty, Freddie Earle, John Abineri, Ex-RSM Brittain, Anita West, Leonard Webb.

The Ray Ellington Quartet; Steve Race and his Orchestra; Orchestrations by Frank Davis; Scripts by Jack Hylton Scripts, Dick Vosburgh and Brad Ashton; Settings by Bernard Carey; Directed by Douglas Hurn.

Alfred Marks is now appearing in *A Day in the Life of...* at the Savoy Theatre London.

(TX 30.3.59)
The sketches are: Spike Milligan as a visiting German General; 'Il Nuovo Telephone', a cod Italian movie; a boxer who plays the tuba and discovers he

has the soul of an artist. The Ray Ellington Quartet perform 'From This Moment On'.

Credits
Appearing with Alfred Marks were Paddie O'Neil, Spike Milligan, Sidney Tafler (now appearing in *Not in the Book* at the Criterion Theatre), Sandra Dorne, Amy Dalby, Michael Balfour, Robert Rietti, John Abineri, Ex-RSM Brittain.

The Ray Ellington Quartet; Steve Race and his Orchestra; Scripts by Jack Hylton Scripts Ltd and Dick Vosburgh and Brad Ashton; Settings by Bernard Carey; Directed by Douglas Hurn.

Alfred Marks and Amy Dalby are appearing in *A Day in The Life Of...* at the Savoy Theatre.

(The *TV Times* credits an appearance by Dick Vosburgh).

Notes
This show was supposed to go out on 16 February 1959 but was withdrawn just before it was due to go out. The picture quality was very poor because there had been lighting problems on set and the programme had been shot with makeshift lights. The sketch with Milligan was considerably shortened because he was so busy with *The Goon Show* he couldn't spare the time to come to rehearsals.

(TX 13.4.59)
The first sketch is about a fairground couple who can't leave their work behind at home. The second is about a busker who becomes a great success as an opera star. Paddie O'Neil and Ray Ellington sing 'Life Is Just a Bowl of Cherries', and Ray sings 'After You've Gone'.

Credits
Appearing with Alfred Marks were Paddie O'Neil, Dulcie Gray, Lonnie Donegan, Irene Handl, Libby Morris, Murray Kash, Therese Burton (now appearing in *A Day in the Life of...* at the Savoy Theatre), Leslie Mitchell, Robert Rietty, Freddie Earle, Ex-RSM Brittain.

The Ray Ellington Quartet; The Barney Gilbraith Singers; Steve Race and his Orchestra; Orchestrations by Alan Braden; Scripts by Dick Vosburgh and Brad Ashton and Eric Merriman and Barry Took; Settings by Bernard Carey; Directed by Douglas Hurn.

Notes
Lonnie Donegan was supposed to be in a sketch about Elizabeth and Essex, but where that went, no-one knows; Brad Ashton doesn't remember Donegan appearing in any such sketch. This is the only show in the series which doesn't use Sid Caesar scripts.

THE ANNE SHELTON SHOW

The series is a mixture of songs and comedy sketches. The first two programmes at the end of 1958 were performed live, but all subsequent episodes were telerecorded.

(TX 5.1.59)
Anne sings 'After You've Gone', 'Let's Call the Whole Thing off' (with Freddie Mills), 'But Not For Me', 'The Man Who Got Away'. Joe Lynch sings 'Rigadoo'. Comedy sketches are a spoof of *Roving Report* and '*Bend the Brain*'.

Cast Anne Shelton, Joe Lynch, Bill Maynard, Thora Hird, Freddie Mills.

Credits
The Beryl Stott Singers; Musical arrangements by Wally Stott and Johnny Spence; Script by Dick Vosburgh and Brad Ashton; Settings by Robert Freemantle; Billy Ternent and his Orchestra; Directed by Bill Hitchcock.

A Jack Hylton Network Production for Associated-Rediffusion.

(TX 12.1.59)
Anne sings 'Brazil', 'Mandolins in the Moonlight' and 'The World Outside' (the theme from *Dangerous Moonlight*), and 'Be a Clown' with Paddie O'Neil. Joe Lynch sings 'Patsy Fagin'. The comedy sketches are about hypnotism and a spoof of the film *Marty*.

Cast Anne Shelton, Terry Scott, Warren Mitchell, Joe Lynch, Alfred Marks, Paddie O'Neil.

Credits
As above.

Alfred Marks is now appearing in *A Day in the Life of* ... at the Savoy Theatre.

(TX 9.2.59)
Anne sings 'Taking A Chance On Love', 'I'll Get By', and 'Lily of Laguna' (with David Tomlinson). Comedy sketches are of two camp hairdressers and a spoof advertising magazine, 'Jim's Creeping Inn'.

Cast Anne Shelton, Warren Mitchell, Harry Fowler, David Tomlinson, Kenneth Connor, Patrick Brawn.

Credits
As above.

(TX 23.2.59)
Anne sings 'I Didn't Know What Time It Was', 'My Blue Heaven' (with Dick Emery and Dick Bentley), 'I.T.A.L.Y.', 'Home Town' (with Bud Flanagan),

'Kiss Me, Kiss Me, Kiss Me', 'Now I Know'. Bud Flanagan sings his latest recording, 'Strollin''. Comedy is provided by two mediums in the interview spot and a musical western version of Shakespeare, 'The Life and Legend of Matt Macbeth'.

Cast Anne Shelton, Bud Flanagan, Dick Bentley, Dick Emery, the Hedley Ward Trio, Patrick Brawn.

Credits
As above.

Notes
The *Daily Sketch* of 24 February 1959 said: 'Dick Bentley was wasted in the Anne Shelton show. I got the impression that he thought his sketches weren't all that funny. He was right. Bud Flanagan — "I was with ENSA in the Crusades" — rescued the programme with a touch of real music-hall gusto.'

(TX 9.3.59)
Anne sings 'It's All Right With Me', 'Suddenly My Heart Sings', 'We Three' (with Kenneth Connor and Edmund Purdom), 'Don't Leave Me Now'. The interview spot is about aviation and the sketch is 'Flo Geste'.

Cast Anne Shelton, Irene Handl, Pat Coombes, Kenneth Connor, Edmund Purdom, Libby Morris, Patrick Brawn.

Credits
The Beryl Stott Singers; Musical arrangements by Wally Stott and Johnny Spence; Script by Dick Vosburgh and Brad Ashton.

Settings by Robert Freemantle; Billy Ternent and his Orchestra; Directed by Michael Westmore.

Notes
Patrick Brawn is uncredited. He had written some of Jack Hylton's earlier shows, for example episodes of *My Husband and I* and Jack Buchanan's series. Dick Vosburgh appears in this show.

(TX 23.3.59)
Anne sings 'We're Having a Heatwave', 'As I Love You', 'It Can't Be Wrong'. The interview spot is about boxing. Anne also meets disc jockeys David Jacobs, Jack Train and Sam Costa, and they sing 'Alright, OK, You Win'. The comedy sketch is a pot pourri of English garden songs.

Cast Anne Shelton, Dick Emery, Graham Stark, Freddie Mills, David Jacobs, Sam Costa, Jack Train, Michael Bentine, Clive Dunn, Patrick Brawn.

Credits
As before.

(TX 6.4.59)
Songs are 'Somebody Loves Me'; a medley of 'On Moonlight Bay', 'Shine on Harvest Moon' and 'Me and My Gal' (with Anne's sister Jo); 'Tread Softly'; 'My Yiddisha Momma'. The interview spot is with two doctors and the sketch is a spoof of '*The Winslow Boy*'.

Cast Anne Shelton, Harry Fowler, Freddie Earle, Jo Shelton, William Russell, Peter Butterworth, Terry Scott, Patrick Brawn, Jimmy Wheeler.

Credits
As before.

Notes
Dick Vosburgh said they wrote this sketch for William Russell, the star of *The Adventures of Sir Lancelot,* as Anne Shelton had a bit of a crush on him at the time.

(TX 20.4.59)
Anne sings 'Tangerine', 'Walk With Faith', 'I Remember it Well' (with Edmund Purdom), 'Fools Rush In', 'In the Still of the Night'. The interview spot is about holidays and the comic sketch tells the story of Bonnie Prince Charlie.

Cast Anne Shelton, Graham Stark, Gladys Morgan, Edmund Purdom, Bill Maynard, Prince Monolulu, Patrick Brawn, Billy Ternent

Credits
As before.

ARTHUR'S ANNIVERSARY
(TX 15.3.57)
A programme which was billed as a celebration of Arthur Askey's thirty years in show business, featuring lots of celebrity guests. In fact, it is just Askey going through a few of his old routines and songs, with the help of daughter Anthea, Danny Ross, and old partner Richard Murdoch. McDonald Hobley appears in a sketch about Napoleon, and Sabrina can be seen briefly at the end. The level of humour can be judged from the fact that the programme ends with Danny Ross getting a custard pie in his face.

Credits
Appearing with Arthur Askey were Anthea Askey, Richard Murdoch, Sabrina, Cameron Hall, Danny Ross and McDonald Hobley (who appears by kind permission of ABC Television Ltd).

Script by Sid Colin; Orchestra conducted by Philip Martell; Setting by Frank Gillman; Assistant to Producer Jean Skinner; Produced and Directed by Eric Fawcett.

A Jack Hylton Production for Associated-Rediffusion

Notes
'Bumpety Bump', a song sung by Askey in this programme, was sung by him in his first professional engagement thirty years previously. Antonia Frazer wrote in the *Evening Standard* of 16 March 1957: 'The occasion was Arthur's 30th anniversary in show business. We were told that everybody out of the top drawer would be there but half an hour later only Richard Murdoch and Sabrina had turned up. ... Anyway he was in splendid form. Old jokes popped like champagne corks.'

BEFORE YOUR VERY EYES
This series had actually begun on BBC television in 1952, with a second series in 1955. Hylton and Askey were old friends, so it was probably obvious that Askey would transfer to ITV for Jack Hylton. Askey probably got more money too, but Anthea Askey recalls that there was generally no contract, just a handshake. Askey was well-used to working in front of a TV camera and was constantly ad libbing and talking directly to the viewers.

(TX 24.2.56)
In the first part of this show Askey introduces Bill Stewart, soon to be his son-in-law. There is a sketch with Askey and Bill Frazer as arctic explorers, and one set in Ancient Troy.

Credits
Before Your Very Eyes with Arthur Askey were Bill Frazer, Anthea Askey, Sabrina, Sam Kydd, Tonia Bern, Totti Truman Taylor, Bill Stewart, Joe Robinson, Graham Leaman. Also taking part Doug Robinson, Roy Siddons, Brian Parker, Timothy Gray.

Musical Direction by Steve Race; Script by Kavanagh Productions Ltd; Settings by Frank Gillman; Directed by Kenneth Carter.

A Jack Hylton Production for Associated-Rediffusion

Notes
Askey comes on at the end to say that they won't be on next Friday as Anthea is getting married. Anthea Askey and Bill Stewart were married on 2 March 1956.

(TX 9.3.56) (Repeated 10.7.56 and 5.5.58)
Includes a sketch set in Richard Murdoch's flat on top of Broadcasting House, and 'The Prince of Puritania' — a spoof on *The Student Prince*.

Credits
Before Your Very Eyes were Richard Murdoch, Bill Frazer, June Whitfield, Sabrina, Mai Bacon, Campbell Gray, Peter White.

The Barney Gilbraith Singers; Guest appearance of Sam Costa; Musical direction by Steve Race; Script by Kavanagh Productions Ltd; Settings by Frank Gillman; Directed by Kenneth Carter.

A Jack Hylton Production for Associated-Rediffusion.
An Associated-Rediffusion Telerecording.

Notes
Philip Purser wrote in the *Daily Mail* of 10 March 1956: 'Arthur Askey took a swipe at the BBC's *At Home* technique and another at Ruritanian operetta. As parodies they were bludgeon-blows rather than rapier strokes, but I laughed a little. By the time Friday comes I need a bludgeon.'

The second repeat transmission of this programme was because Askey's ill-health forced the cancellation of the scheduled programme and this was a last minute substitute, instead of a hastily put-together live alternative.

During the end credits of the 35mm print, Askey comes on to say 'ta ta' to the viewers, but the print is cut. On the 16mm print he says they are on next week, then the week after, then two weeks after that. Meanwhile there are more 'goons' at ten o'clock. This is probably a reference to *Idiot Weekly Price 2d* which followed later in the evening on the original transmission of 9 March 1956. The 35mm print is probably cut before the reference to *Idiot Weekly* because it was the repeat version.

(TX 23.3.56)
Arthur Askey presents, and says it's the end of the show, rolling the credits (through a mangle). He says they were faded out the week before so they decided to do the end first. Sketches include one about a Summer Fayre, with Jerry Desmonde as the vicar and Askey as 'Miss Prim', and a spoof of *House of Wax*.

Credits
Before Your Very Eyes were Jerry Desmonde, Sabrina, Tom Mennard, Faith Bailey, Kenneth Seeger, Elisse Relnah, Joy Harvey, Hazel Johns, and Andrew Fenner at the organ.

Scripts by Kavanagh Productions Ltd; Musical Direction by Steve Race; Settings by Frank Gillman. The producers wish to express their thanks to Madame Tussauds for their kind co-operation. Directed by Kenneth Carter.

A Jack Hylton Production for Associated-Rediffusion

Notes
In the *News Chronicle* of March 22 1956, James Thomas reported that the waxworks loaned by Tussaud's were Mrs Flanagan, a murderess who usually

stood next to Crippen, and former diplomats, who would be heavily disguised, so as not to offend. Mrs Flanagan was insured for £500.

(TX 6.4.56) REPEATED 17.7.56
The first sketch is about two escaped criminals, the second a spoof of *The Three Musketeers*. Part two of the programme has no sound.

Credits
Jerry Desmonde, Sabrina, Tom Gill, Fanny Carby, Ray Browne, Peter White, Ernie Brooks.

Script by Kavanagh Productions Ltd; Musical Direction by Steve Race; Settings by Frank Gillman.
The Producers wish to express their thanks to the 2nd Edgware Boy Scouts Troop (St Margarets) and the Boy Scouts Association for their co-operation. Directed by Kenneth Carter.

(TX 20.4.56)
Sketches are set in a Government Vehicle Testing Station and a Hollywood film studio.

Credits
Jerry Desmonde, Avril Angers, Sabrina, John Blythe, Ray Browne, Richard Klee, Neale Warrington, Gloria Gaynor.

Script by Kavanagh Productions Ltd; Musical Direction by Steve Race; Settings by Frank Gillman; Directed by Kenneth Carter.

(TX 2.12.57)
Sketches include one about method acting, and a spoof of *The Prisoner of Zenda*.

Credits
June Whitfield, Alun Owen and Tom Gill, David Nettheim, Jimmy Green, John Dunbar, Billy Martin, Jimmy Scott and Walter's Dogs.

Billy Ternent and his Orchestra; Script by Sid Colin and Talbot Rothwell; Settings by Michael Yates; Directed by Kenneth Carter.

Notes
The show was telerecorded because Askey had pantomime rehearsals. It ranked 11th in TAM ratings with 63, watched in 2,892,000 homes. A rating of 63 meant that 63 per cent of televisions were tuned to this programme.

(TX 16.12.57)
Includes 'Frankenstein' and 'Great Composers' sketches.

June Whitfield, Alun Owen and John Bailey, Sheena Marshe, David Nettheim, Graham Lines, Golda Casimir and Arthur Askey.

Orchestra under the direction of Norman Whitehead; Script by Sid Colin and Talbot Rothwell; Settings by Henry Federer; Directed by Kenneth Carter.

Notes
This was Kenneth Carter's last show as an AR-TV staff member. Alun Owen became a writer, and his credits included the classic Wednesday Play drama *Lena, O My Lena* and the Beatles film *A Hard Day's Night*. 4th in TAM ratings with a rating of 67.

THE CRAZY GANG'S PARTY
(TX 23.12.57)
The 'party' is a strange mixture of Crazy Gang sketches and studio and film guest inserts. Donald Campbell appears in a brief, rather fuzzy film clip, and Sir Robert Boothby in a spoof about Nato. Flanagan and Allen sing 'Down Every Street' and Jimmy Wheeler, Harry Green and Jack Solomons appear in sketches. Peter Glaze and Arthur Askey play genies.

Credits
At Home The Crazy Gang, Nervo and Knox, Bud Flanagan, Naughton and Gold and 'Monsewer' Eddie Gray. *The Guests* Chesney Allen, Arthur Askey, Sir Robert Boothby MP, Donald Campbell, Peter Glaze, Alfred Marks, Jack Solomons, Jimmy Wheeler, Harry Green.

Musical Director Billy Ternent; Devised and written by Bud Flanagan; Directed by Michael Westmore.

Notes
There had been a lot of publicity in the press about the Gang doing their skit on Cheam School, where Prince Charles was a pupil. It had apparently been a hit at the Royal Variety Performance and should have been in this programme. There was quite a fuss when it wasn't shown, but apparently Flanagan decided that at eight minutes it was too long. The Nato sketch, called 'The Diplomats', had also appeared in the Royal Variety Performance, with Brian Reece playing the part taken by Bob Boothby.

There was a lot of internal conflict about this programme. The rather strange laughter is because there was not enough room in the studio for an audience, so director Michael Westmore asked permission for a laughter track to be laid. There is no laughter track on the NFTVA's copy, just the laughter of what must be presumed to be the crew and hangers-on.

The jumps in the film were there on transmission. Orders were given by Lloyd Williams, A-R's Director of Production, to cut out torn sprocket holes rather than await the arrival of reprints and have the editor cut them in before transmission.

THE CYRIL FLETCHER SHOW

(TX 9.4.59)
The programme is a collection of sketches, with Fletcher, Betty Astell and Pat Coombs. Shani Wallis sings 'You Make Me Feel So Young' and 'I Know Why and So Do You'. Jack Tripp appears in a comic ballet of 'The Dance of the Hours'. All sketches are accompanied by raucous laughter, which often drowns the punchlines.

Credits
Artists appearing were Cyril Fletcher, Betty Astell, Pat Coombs, Jack Tripp, Shani Wallis.

Musical Director Bill Ternent; Settings by Denis Wreford; Directed by Milo Lewis.

The *TV Times* credits: Ian Francis, Ian Wilson; Scripts by Johnny Speight.

A Jack Hylton Network Production for Associated-Rediffusion from London.

Notes
Philip Purser wrote in the *News Chronicle* of 10 April 1959: 'Hylton strikes again! A brand new show this time, *The Cyril Fletcher Show*, but with most of the old Hylton house marks on it. Where do they find that maniacal studio audience? How do they get that special tinned flavour, as though the programme had been stored at the back of a cupboard for a fortnight? ... Shani Wallis survived one of the ugliest costumes ever worn on TV. The rest had better be silence.'

Jack Tripp's 'guest appearance' is lifted from excerpts Hylton shot for his first TV shows in 1955.

THE DICKIE HENDERSON HALF-HOUR

These programmes were very popular with the public and went down quite well with some critics. Dickie and Anthea were supposed to be a married couple who appear to spend all their time bickering, mis-understanding each other and arguing. In these sketches the women are always scatty, while the men are usually the archetypal 'little man' battling against the world and coming off worst. The sketches are from Sid Caesar's *Your Show of Shows*, which were secretly bought by Hylton on his and A-R's behalf. All programmes begin with Henderson dancing on top of the show's titles. Some of the soundtracks are incomplete.

(TX 11.7.58)
Sketches include taking the new baby for a walk in the park; visiting a fortune teller; trying to get served in a busy café. Ilene Day sings 'Sometimes I'm Happy' and 'Worriation'.

Credits
Dickie Henderson (Appearing by kind permission of Bernard Delfont), Anthea Askey, Eve Lister, Bernard Hunter, Freddie Mills, Ilene Day.

Settings by Robert Freemantle; Film Editor Jack Giggs; Steve Race and his Orchestra; Directed by Bill Hitchcock.

TV Times credits: Material by Jack Greenhalgh.

A Jack Hylton Network Production for Associated-Rediffusion

Notes
Twenty years previously Dickie Henderson had been props boy with the Jack Hylton Band. This programme came 6th in the TAM ratings with 51, watched in 2,913,000 homes

(TX 18.7.58)
Sketches are: getting tickets for a show but being too near the band; trying to carry on a conversation with someone you think you know but can't place; 'Hate', a cod-French romantic film. Diane Todd sings 'I'll Take Romance'.

Credits
Dickie Henderson (Appearing by kind permission of Bernard Delfont), Anthea Askey, Eve Lister, Bernard Hunter, Eric Delaney, Diane Todd, Len Lowe.

Settings by Robert Freemantle; Steve Race and his Orchestra; Directed by Bill Hitchcock.

TV Times credits: Material by Jack Greenhalgh.

A Jack Hylton Network Production for Associated-Rediffusion.

Notes
The *Daily Mail* 'Teleview' of 19 July 1958 said: 'Last night the stylish racon-teur of the Sunday Palladium Show polished off two sketches that would not have disgraced Sid Caesar'. Little did they know ... Ranked 4th in TAM ratings with 52; watched in 3,077,000 homes.

(TX 25.7.58)
Sketches are: what happens when Anthea hires a butler; 'A Drunkard's Fate', a spoof silent film. Jill Day sings 'Easy To Remember'.

Credits
Dickie Henderson (Appearing by kind permission of Bernard Delfont), Anthea Askey, Eve Lister, Bernard Hunter, Jill Day, Len Lowe.

Settings by Robert Freemantle; Steve Race and his Orchestra; Directed by Bill Hitchcock.

TV Times credits: Material by Jack Greenhalgh.

Notes
This show was put back from 8.30 p.m. to 10.15 p.m. because of the Empire Games.

(TX 1.8.58)
Sketches are: Anthea is always contradicting and correcting Dickie when he tries to tell a story; what happens to the cricket commentary when rain stops play; how Dickie suffers when Anthea is on a diet. Pat Moore sings 'Love Is Where You Find It'.

Credits
Dickie Henderson (Appearing by kind permission of Bernard Delfont), Anthea Askey, Eve Lister, Bernard Hunter, Len Lowe, Sara Leighton, Patricia Moore.

Settings by Robert Freemantle; Film Editor Jack Giggs; Steve Race and his Orchestra; Directed by Bill Hitchcock.

Notes
Twenty-two-year-old Pat Moore's brief career had been as an understudy in two musicals until she was given an audition by Jack Hylton. The show was 9th in TAM ratings with 45; watched in 2,740,000 homes

(TX 8.8.58)
The first sketch tells how turbulent Dickie and Anthea's relationship was even before they got married, the second is about betting too much at an auction, then the visit of loud Texan relatives. Marion Keene sings 'Taking a Chance on Love'.

Credits
Dickie Henderson (Appearing by kind permission of Bernard Delfont), Anthea Askey, Eve Lister, Bernard Hunter, Guest star William Sylvester (now appearing in *The Joshua Tree* at the Duke of York's Theatre), Len Lowe, Sara Leighton.

Settings by Robert Freemantle; Film Editor Jack Giggs; Steve Race and his Orchestra; Directed by Bill Hitchcock.

TV Times credits Grace Webb.

Notes
This episode contains an uncredited appearance as the maid by Patsy Rowlands. It ranked 6th in TAM ratings with 55; watched in 3,002,000 homes.

(TX 15.8.58)
The first sketch is 'Business As Usual', about a young executive who collapses because he is working too hard. The second sketch, 'A Night Out with the Boys' has no sound. Ilene Day sings 'I Get a Kick Out of You'.

Credits
Dickie Henderson (Appearing by kind permission of Bernard Delfont), Anthea Askey, Eve Lister, Bernard Hunter, Freddie Mills, Len Lowe, John Abineri, Ilene Day.

Settings by Robert Freemantle; Film Editor Jack Giggs; Steve Race and his Orchestra; Directed by Bill Hitchcock.

(TX 22.8.58)
Sketches are: going for a drive in the country with friends; going out for an expensive meal; what happens when Dickie can't sleep. Diane Todd sings 'Bali Hi'.

Credits
Dickie Henderson (Appearing by kind permission of Bernard Delfont), Anthea Askey, Eve Lister, Bernard Hunter, Freddie Mills, Diane Todd.

Settings by Robert Freemantle; Film Editor Jack Giggs; Steve Race and his Orchestra; Directed by Bill Hitchcock.

(TX 29.8.58)
Sketches are: Anthea worries about getting old; spring cleaning; 'Cat on a Hot Tin Streetcar'. Marion Keene sings 'Day by Day'.

Credits
Dickie Henderson (Appearing by kind permission of Bernard Delfont), Anthea Askey, Eve Lister, Bernard Hunter, Marion Keene.

Settings by Robert Freemantle; Film Editor Jack Giggs; Steve Race and his Orchestra; Directed by Bill Hitchcock.

(TX 5.9.58)
The first sketch is about Anthea forgetting to pass on messages, the second is 'Homicide 65300', a thriller where music is supposed to add the drama that is missing from the story. The spoof credits at the begining are the names of real people working for Jack Hylton or A-R, such as John Russell, Frank Holland, Bob Swash, Diana Parry, Vic Sullivan. Marion Keene sings the opening song.

Credits
Dickie Henderson (Appearing by kind permission of Bernard Delfont), Anthea Askey, Eve Lister, Bernard Hunter, Marion Keene.

Settings by Robert Freemantle; Billy Ternent and his Orchestra; Directed by Bill Hitchcock.

A Jack Hylton Network Production for Associated-Rediffusion.

Ranked 10th in the TAM ratings with 46; Watched in 2,792,000 homes.

(TX 12.9.58)
Dickie introduces the last show of the series. The first sketch is about what happens when a husband and wife don't have the same sense of humour. The second is about what happens when an attractive blonde moves in next door, and the third is a spoof silent movie, 'The Love Bandit'. Diane Todd sings 'Beloved'.

*Credits (*from the *TV Times)*
Dickie Henderson, Anthea Askey, Bernard Hunter, Eve Lister, June Cunningham, Diane Todd.

Settings by Robert Freemantle; Billy Ternent and His Orchestra; Directed by Bill Hitchcock.

Notes
Ranked 4th in the TAM ratings; watched in 3,900,000 homes.

(TX 4.5.59)
The first sketch is about moving house, the second is set in the boardroom of the Henderson Novelty Company. Dickie sings 'Got The World on a String' and Marion Keene sings 'Day by Day'.

Credits
Dickie Henderson (Appearing by kind permission of Bernard Delfont), Anthea Askey, Eve Lister, Bernard Hunter, Clive Dunn, Marion Keene.

Billy Ternent and his Orchestra; Script Associate Jimmy Grafton; Settings by Denis Wreford; Directed by Bill Hitchcock.

(TX 11.5.59)
Sketches are: getting phone messages muddled up; Dickie and Anthea as little children; a spoof silent movie, 'The Sewing Machine Girl'. Dickie sings 'It All Depends on You', Marion Keene sings 'You Make Me Feel So Young', Dickie and Anthea sing 'Thank Heaven For Little Girls'.

Credits
As above.

(TX 18.5.59)
The first sketch concerns an argument about doing the dishes, the second is about trying to get a seat at a quick lunch counter. Dickie sings 'Come to My Arms', which he wrote himself, and Renate Holm sings 'Summertime'.

Credits
No credits but as above except for Renate Holm, instead of Marion Keene.

Renate Holm had been on an edition of Jack Hylton's *Focus on Youth*. The Hylton office had apparently been inundated with mail asking to see her again.

(TX 25.5.59)
The first sketch is about hiring a maid, the second is a spoof B movie, 'The Petrified Hours'. Dickie sings 'Breezing Along with the Breeze'.

Credits
Dickie Henderson (Appearing by kind permission of Bernard Delfont), Anthea Askey, Eve Lister, Bernard Hunter. Guest Artist Lionel Murton.

Billy Ternent and His Orchestra; Script Associate Jimmy Grafton; Settings by Denis Wreford; Directed by Bill Hitchcock.

(TX 1.6.59)
No sound for the first part, which is a sketch about having toothache. The second sketch is about Dickie and Anthea celebrating their tenth wedding anniversary and arguing over details. They finish by singing 'I Remember It Well'.

Credits
As 18.5.59.

(TX 8.6.59)
The first sketch is about Anthea's embarrassing new hairstyle. Dickie sings 'Just In Time'. No sound for second part. Marion Keene sings 'That Old Feeling'. The sketch is 'One Track Mind'.

Credits
As 18.5.59.

(TX 15.6.59)
The first sketch is about buying a dog, the second concerns standing in the wrong queue in the Post Office. Dickie sings 'It's Almost Like Being In Love' and Marion Keene sings 'When I Fall In Love'.

Credits
As 18.5.59.

Notes
Uncredited appearance in the 'Post Office' sketch by Ronnie Corbett.

FRIDAY NIGHT WITH THE CRAZY GANG
(TX 5.10.56)
The programme contains dancing from the Tiller Girls and songs from Rosalina Neri, including '*A Frangesa!*' and 'You Made Me Love You'. The

Crazy Gang perform various crossover routines, a comedy balloon dance, 'Tedwardian Nights' and 'The Scarlet Pimpernel'.

Credits
With the Crazy Gang were Rosalina Neri, The Tiller Girls under the direction of Barbara Aitken. Billy Ternent and His Orchestra; Director of Photography Gerald Moss; Supervising Editor Frank Cadman; Production Manager for Jack Hylton John Russell.

TV Times credits: Musical direction by Cyril Ornadel. Directed by Michael Westmore.

A Jack Hylton Production for Associated-Rediffusion.

Notes
This programme was filmed at the Adelphi Theatre on 26, 27 and 28 September 1956. Most of the material was from the *Jokers Wild* revue at the Victoria Palace. The 'Tedwardian Nights' routine is based on a Robert Dhéry sketch. The original Dhéry sketch can be seen in *The Robert Dhéry Show* (22 March 1957).

A lot of the acts had been seen in *Jack Hylton Presents* (24 April 1956). The 'Crossovers', 'Tedwardian Nights' and *Scarlet Pimpernel* sketches were all done on the earlier show, but this was only seen in the London region.

The telerecording was repeated on 23 June 1958 as *Jack Hylton's Monday Show*, owing to the fact that the Hylton organisation was unable to do the live Arthur Askey programme they had planned. The 1958 repeat got a TAM rating of 41, watched in 2,331,000 homes.

GAY OPERETTA
Hylton was not happy at having to present these potted operettas in such a short slot when he had gone to the trouble of securing the services of the Sadlers Wells Opera Company. However, he had very little choice as the half-hour slot was the only one open to him. The series was his attempt to add a little bit of culture to his programming.

COUNTESS MARITZA
(TX 6.11.59)
Emmerich Kalman's operetta gets the Jack Hylton treatment.

Credits
Devised by Dudley Glass; Lyrics by Arthur Stanley; Introduced by Derek Oldham.

By arrangement with Sadlers Wells Trust those appearing were:
Countess Maritza   Victoria Elliot

Tassilo	William McAlpine
Lisa	Margaret Nisbett
Populescu	Eric Shilling
Cheko	Stanley Beedle
Manja	Deidree Thurlow

The Sadlers Wells Orchestra, Conductor William Reid; Members of The Sadlers Wells Chorus and Opera Ballet; Choreography by Philippe Perrottet; Designed by Denis Wreford; Directed by Mark Lawton.

A Jack Hylton Network Production for Associated-Rediffusion from London.

THE MERRY WIDOW
(TX 13.11.59)
Franz Lehar's operetta in twenty-five minutes.

Credits
Devised by Dudley Glass; English Lyrics by Christopher Hassal; Introduced by Derek Oldham.

By arrangement with Sadlers Wells Trust those appearing were:

Anna Glavari	June Bronhill
Count Danilo	Peter Grant
Valencienne	Marion Lowe
Baron Zeta	Howell Glynne
Camille	Rowland Jones
Cascada	Frederick Sharp
St Brioche	John Kentish

The Sadlers Wells Orchestra, Conductor William Reid; Members of The Sadlers Wells Chorus and Opera Ballet; Choreography Philippe Perrottet; Designed by Denis Wreford; Directed by Mark Lawton.

THE GIPSY BARON
(TX 27.11.59)
The Sadlers Wells Opera company whizz through Strauss's operetta in twenty-five minutes.

Credits
Devised by Dudley Glass; Lyrics by Henrik Ege; Introduced by Derek Oldham.

By arrangement with Sadlers Wells Trust those appearing were:

Barinkay	Alexander Young
Saffi	Joan Stuart
Zsupan	Howell Glynne

Czipra	Sheila Rex
Arsena	Nancy Creighton
Homonay	John Hargreaves

The Sadlers Wells Orchestra, Conductor William Reid; Members of the Sadlers Wells Chorus and Opera Ballet; Choreography by Philippe Perrottet; Designed by Denis Wreford; Directed by Mark Lawton.

Notes
Punch, 18 November 1959: 'In a fuzzy, surrealist way I found the half-hour potted version of *Countess Maritza* — one of a series called *Gay Operetta* — extremely amusing. There were the absurd costumes, which always make romps of this kind look like an office party in a firm of theatrical costumiers ... there were a lot of what I took to be madly roistering gipsies, whose demeanour seemed more appropriate to members of an English wedding party made sedately frivolous by a couple of sherries. ... Mr Jack Hylton, who presents the series, certainly seems to have tapped a rich mine of crazy comedy here.'

GERT AND DAISY

Gert and Daisy, characters invented and played by Elsie and Doris Waters, are two performers who now run a theatrical boarding house. Each week they invite viewers to find out what they and their guests have been up to. The main guests are Hugh Paddick and Patsy Rowlands as Boris and Bonnie. This series was shot without a studio audience.

(TX 10.8.59)
In this episode the ladies and their lodgers decide to go on a diet. The rather strange one they choose means, inevitably, that they all sneak down to the kitchen at night time, in order to raid the larder.

Credits
Gert and Daisy's Guests were
Boris	Hugh Paddick
Bonnie	Patsy Rowlands
Lulu	Jennifer Browne
Maureen	Dudy Nimmo
Harry	Julian D'Albie
Violet	Rosemary Scott
Rod	Keith Faulkner
The Raindrops

Script by Ted Willis; Settings by Denis Wreford; Directed by Milo Lewis.

Notes
Newspaper reports say that Ted Willis got the idea for this series while relaxing in his armchair watching TV. He saw Gert and Daisy in a commercial and

wondered why someone didn't write a series for them. He then decided he could write one himself. The series didn't go down well with the critics, who thought it old-fashioned and unfunny. It was around this time that Hylton productions were reaching a low point and Hylton was taking a great deal of flak in the press.

(TX 17.8.59)
There is trouble when it seems that Lulu, who suddenly has lots of extra cash, might be a cat burglar. Although this leads to hilarious antics, the real culprit is eventually apprehended and Lulu is able to go off to a fancy dress ball dressed as a burglar.

Credits
Boris	Hugh Paddick
Bonnie	Patsy Rowlands
Lulu	Jennifer Browne
Maureen	Dudy Nimmo
Harry	Julian d'Albie
Violet	Rosemary Scott
PC Fred	Frank Pettitt
Malcolm	Patrick Godfrey
Sergeant	Raymond Adamson

Script by Lew Schwarz; Devised by Ted Willis; Settings by Denis Wreford; Directed by Milo Lewis.

(TX 24.8.59)
This is the saddest episode in the series. Bonnie and Boris have finally got an engagement, but all is not rosy for Harry and Violet. It is their thirtieth wedding anniversary, but it will be the first time they haven't been working on that date, so they don't want to celebrate. Gert and Daisy agree to appear for impresario Jack Parmont if he will book Harry and Violet. It soon becomes clear why Harry and Vi aren't working – they're absolutely dreadful. Gert and Daisy have to resort to buying all the tickets for the show and arranging a coach to bring all their old friends up from London. Added to that, there is a routine from a couple of novelty dancers who were probably there to fill out the time slot.

Credits (taken from *TV Times*)
Hugh Paddick, Patsy Rowlands, Dudy Nimmo, Jennifer Browne, Julian d'Albie, Rosemary Scott, The Lynton Boys, Thomas Gallagher.

Billy Miller and his Orchestra; Devised by Ted Willis; Written by Lew Schwartz; Settings by Denis Wreford; Directed by Milo Lewis.

Notes
Peter Black wrote in the *Daily Mail* of 25 August 1959: 'Lew Schwartz, a modern writer for television, joined Jack Hylton to write last night's script for the *Gert and Daisy Show* and hit off the style of the 1929 talking picture to a hair. How does Hylton do it?'

(TX 31.8.59)
Gert and Daisy and their guests decide to try and convince Maureen's father that she is just about to make it big, to stop him taking her back home.

Credits
Boris   Hugh Paddick
Bonnie   Patsy Rowlands
Howard Scott   John Salew
Lulu   Jennifer Browne
Maureen   Dudy Nimmo
Harry   Julian d'Albie
Violet   Rosemary Scott
Rod   Keith Faulkner

Script by Malcolm A. Hulke and Eric Paice; Devised by Ted Willis; Settings by Denis Wreford; Directed by Milo Lewis.

(TX 7.9.59)
Gert and Daisy decide to go on an economy drive, but so bizarre are the ways they all try and save money that they end up out of pocket. The most far-fetched idea involves the use of a goat!

Credits
Boris   Hugh Paddick
Bonnie   Patsy Rowlands
Lulu   Jennifer Browne
Maureen   Dudy Nimmo
Harry   Julian D'Albie
Violet   Rosemary Scott
Delivery Boy   Robin Kildare

Script by Malcolm A. Hulke and Eric Paice; Devised by Ted Willis; Settings by Denis Wreford; Directed by Milo Lewis.

(TX 16.9.59)
An old newspaper discovered under the stair carpet has an article which implies that Boris is an Archduke. They start treating him like royalty, and Boris, once he discovers what they think, is happy to go along with it.

Credits
Boris   Hugh Paddick
Bonnie   Patsy Rowlands
Lulu   Jennifer Browne
Maureen   Dudy Nimmo
Harry   Julian D'Albie

| Violet | Rosemary Scott |
| Malcolm | Patrick Godfrey |

Script by Malcolm A. Hulke and Eric Paice; Devised by Ted Willis; Settings by Denis Wreford; Directed by Milo Lewis.

HOTEL RIVIERA
(TX 2.8.57)
This series was an attempt to add a touch of continental sophistication to the summer schedules. It was set in a hotel on the French Riviera and had a running storyline, as well as lots of musical interludes from Rosalina Neri. Alec d'Arcy is supposed to be the hotel manager, Bentley a visitor and Neri a cabaret artist appearing at the hotel.

The first part of this programme has no picture, only sound. In part two Rosa sings 'You Do Something to Me'/'You Made Me Love You' and later dances with a little man in glasses and waves a floaty scarf around. There are various sub-plots built around a character who may or may not be a Maharajah.

Credits
Dick Bentley, Alec d'Arcy, Rosalina Neri, Tom Gill, Peter Wyngarde, Tony Shaw, Glen Alyn, John Whyte.

Dances arranged by Ross Taylor; Orchestra under the direction of Billy Ternent; Script by David Climie; Settings by Fred Pusey; Produced by Richard Bird; Directed by Peter Croft.

Notes
This episode was probably recorded because Rosalina was going on holiday. It was telerecorded on 23 July 1957 at the Wembley studios. This series is supposed to be terribly glamorous, but it's all shot on the usual sort of sets and seems more like a vehicle for Rosalina Neri. It alternated with *Beside the Seaside*, also starring Bentley, with Glenn Melvyn and Danny Ross. Much play was made in the press at the time of Rosa returning to Italy after the first episode, to appear on TV in Milan, for the first time since she was banned for being too sexy. TV critics thought she was the best thing in the show even though she sometimes mimed her songs.

Alec d'Arcy had been in continental films in the late 20s and early 30s and had then gone to America. His most famous appearance would be in *How to Marry a Millionaire*. According to Hylton files, Sheila Steafel was one of the extras, for which she received £3.

JACK HYLTON'S MONDAY SHOW
This was a general title for whatever happened to be going out in Hylton's Monday night spot. It was usually half an hour of variety.

(TX 10.2.58)
A mixture of comedy and music, hosted by Dick Bentley. Leonard Weir sings 'The Sunshine of Your Smile', Jimmy Wheeler and Tommy Fields play 'Around The World' on their violins. Rosalina Neri sings and dances with Lionel Blair and then sings '*La Vie en Rose*' and '*Arrivederci Roma*'. Neri and Blair sing and dance 'Give My Regards to Broadway'. The Three Buffoons do a dance routine dressed as clowns. Wheeler, Bentley and Fields do a comedy routine with violins. Neri and Weir sing '*Santa Lucia*'.

Credits
Dick Bentley introduced Rosalina Neri, Jimmy Wheeler, Tommy Fields, Leonard Weir, The Radio Revellers, The Buffoons, Lionel Blair, Mary Reynolds, Margaret Lee, Ian Kaye, Robert Lamont.

Musical Director Billy Ternent; Dances arranged by Lionel Blair; Settings by Frank Nerini; Directed by Bill Hitchcock.

Notes
Jimmy Wheeler and Tommy Fields had just finished appearing in panto together. Rosalina Neri was out of the country, supposedly singing the lead in *L'Elisir d'amore* in Italy, and this is given as the excuse for telerecording.

The *Weekly Sporting Review* of 14 February 1958 quotes Jimmy Wheeler: 'What an amazing impresario Hylton is, in the real sense of the word, always there keeping an eye on things in the background'. Tommy Fields was Gracie's brother.

(TX 17.2.58)
A variety show with a difference, this was presented from a BOAC Britannia aeroplane flying from London to New York while a selection of guests performed musical numbers, or talked to Hughie Green about their reason for being on the flight. The sound for the musical numbers has been lost but one piece, obviously the only one actually performed live on the aircraft, survives. This is a four-year-old girl called Helen, who talks to Hughie Green, then sings 'Around The World' and plays the trumpet, accompanied by Jack Hylton himself on the piano.

No credits, but
Hughie Green, Paddy Stone, Donald Campbell, Laurence Harvey, Winifred Atwell, Ronnie Ronalde, Rosalina Neri, Jack Hylton, Captain Percy (captain of the aircraft).

TV Times credits:
Billy Ternent and his Orchestra; Paddy Stone and his dancers; Written by Jimmy Coghill; Film director Ted Lloyd; Associate producer Bimbi Harris.

Notes
There had obviously been a great deal of publicity from the Hylton offices about this, but the newspapers weren't really impressed. Helen was Helen

Crayford, aged four, from Broadstairs, Kent. Philip Purser wrote in the *News Chronicle* of 18 February 1958: 'The main thing established by Hughie Green's programme filmed aboard a transatlantic airliner was that what would have been a dud show at sea level was still a dud show at 32,000 feet'.

Ramsden Grieg said in the *Evening Standard* of 18 February 1958: 'I am now wondering when I can expect to see Val Parnell's *Sunday Night at the London Palladium* presented from the top deck of a No. 13 bus'. The 'coloured musical' talked about by Laurence Harvey is *Simply Heavenly*, which was showcased in *Jack Hylton's Monday Show* of 26 May 1958.

The Hylton TV Committee thoroughly enjoyed the programme! The musical items were obviously pre-recorded, though they have not survived. The complete transmission soundtrack went missing somewhere between Hylton House and Television House in 1958. The programme achieved a TAM rating of 49; watched in 2,404,000 homes

(TX 3.3.58) aka A DAY IN NEW YORK
A programme filmed in New York, where Hughie Green's interviews with celebrities and two GI brides are interspersed with Paddy Stone dance sequences. Patti Lewis sings 'How About You'.

TV Times Credits
Hughie Green with Peter Ustinov, Mary Ure, Patti Lewis, Alec Templeton, Dr Ralph Bunche, Paddy Stone

Written by Jimmy Coghill; Directed by Bimbi Harris.

Notes
The *Daily Mirror* of 3 March 1958 has an article which states that Hughie Green forgot to ask the GI Brides's maiden names or the addresses of their families, so no one was able to contact them and warn them to watch the programme. Their married names were Jenny Martin and Peggy Farini.

A letter in the *TV Times* of 14 March 1958 asks who the 'repulsive schoolgirl' is in the *Monday Show*. She is fifteen-year-old Hazel Foster, and Hughie Green answers that she is just part of the atmosphere as they are trying to do an off-beat show.

The minutes of the Jack Hylton Television Production Committee meeting held on 7 March 1958 record that all the members agreed that it was a bad show. Bob Swash went on record as saying it was: 'An inferior documentary programme, badly produced.' Hylton had joined this meeting and said that he would write to Hughie Green complaining about the programme. The complaints are probably to do with the technical quality, which is very poor and the sound is badly out of sync. Achieved a TAM rating of 40; watched in 2,136,000 homes.

(TX 7.4.58)
Another mixure of comedy and music, hosted by Dick Bentley. Leonard Weir sings 'Belonging to Someone', and Rosalina Neri sings '*La Panse*' and '*Chella*

La'. Dick Bentley gets stuck in yoga positions in between musical numbers. Weir and Neri sing a duet from *La Traviata*. Leo Bassi and June juggle objects with their feet. Dick Bentley and Rosalina Neri sing 'In Your Easter Bonnet'. This is the last show in the series and finishes with Rosalina singing '*Souvenir d'Italie*'.

Credits
Dick Bentley introduced Rosalina Neri, Leonard Weir, Leo Bassi and June, Peter Reeves, Lizabeth Page, Lionel Blair, Margaret Lee, Judy Carne, Ian Kaye, Robert Lamont, Mavis Ascott, Ina Clare, Jane Hunt, Audrey Hodgkiss.

Dances arranged by Lionel Blair; Script by Eric Merriman and Barry Took; Musical Associate Billy Miller; Billy Ternent and his Orchestra; Settings by Frank Nerini; Directed by Bill Hitchcock.

Notes
June, of Leo Bassi and June, is Jimmy Wheeler's daughter. In a letter to Mr William Wyatt, Bob Swash confirms that in the show on 27 January 1958 the Neri/Weir duet was mimed: 'to give greater freedom of movement to the artistes, but after they had previously recorded this number themselves'. It looks as though their duet in this programme is mimed too.

(TX 26.5.58)
The theme of this show is 'The Theatre'. Paddy Stone performs a *Dragnet* ballet. Green talks to his godfather, Bransby Williams. Vanessa Lee sings 'I Can Give You the Starlight'. Green, Lee and Billy Ternent sing and dance 'S'Wonderful'. Laurence Harvey talks about *Simply Heavenly* by Langston Hughes, which he is directing at the Adelphi. David Martin, Bertice Reading and John Bouie perform a number from the show.

Credits
Hughie Green's Guests: Laurence Harvey, Vanessa Lee, Bransby Williams, Bertice Reading, David Martin, Paddy Stone, with Tanya Duray, Jo Williamson, Judy Horn, Bryan Ryman, Bill Haydon, and Ian Kaye.

Choreography by Paddy Stone; Orchestra conducted by Billy Ternent; Designed by Robert Freemantle; Script by Jimmy Coghill and Bill Smith; Directed by Eric J. Croall.

Notes
Achieved a TAM rating of 29; watched in 1,629,000 homes

JACK HYLTON PRESENTS
A title which covered the various mixed variety programmes which went out in Hylton's slots

(TX 4.10.55)
'Jack Hylton Proudly Presents the Musical Surprise of the Year — introduced by Larry Adler'. Larry Adler introduces Xavier Cugat, the King of the Mambo. The rest of the programme is Cugat and his band playing a selection of Latin American tunes, including the new Cuban rhythm 'Cha Cha Cha'. Cugat's wife, Abbe Lane, sings and dances, and Rosita Alonso performs a flamenco dance.

There are no end credits.

Notes
Cugat was appearing in Paris at the time, and this was filmed there about 21 September 1955, possibly in different versions for sale elsewhere. The leader on this film said 'English Version'. Philip Purser's review in the *Daily Mail* of 5th October 1955 mentions an opening *paso doble*, which is not in this film, and also a 'Spanish' comic, who is also missing from the film. According to the Hylton contracts, Mercedes & Triana and Bernard Spear were live in the studio, so these are perhaps the live studio parts mentioned by Purser.

(TX 24.5.56)
This is part of the Crazy Gang's stage revue *Jokers Wild*, recorded on 23 May 1956 before a live audience at the Victoria Palace Theatre. It seems to have been recorded very quickly, over one hour from 6.30 p.m. to 7.30 p.m. Shows were twice nightly, at 6.15 p.m. and 8.45 p.m., so there would have been no other time, unless the first evening performance on that day was cancelled.

Songs and sketches include Josephine Anne and the John Tiller Girls in a Helen of Troy song and dance routine; the saucy 'Hotel Splendide' sketch; Bob and Marion Konyott, a comedy acrobatic act; 'What's My Line', where the Gang parody Ron Randell, Isobel Barnett, Barbara Kelly and Gilbert Harding; a solo spot by Bud Flanagan, during which he tells gags and sings 'Mr Sandman' and 'I Belong To London', before being joined by the 'boys and girls' of the company; a 'British Railways' sketch with the Gang dressed as charwomen, except for Knox, who is a tea lady.

Credits
The Crazy Gang with Bob and Marion Konyot, Josephine Anne, Vera Day, Peter Glaze, The Carden Dancers, The John Tiller Girls.

Victoria Palace Orchestra under the direction of Ronnie Munro; Comedy directed by Charles Henry; Music and lyrics by Ross Parker; Dances and Musical Numbers arranged by George Carden; Staged by Alec Shanks; Directed for Television by Michael Westmore.

Notes
This programe is a very good example of what the Crazy Gang must have been like on stage. The atmosphere of the theatre is well conveyed, especially

in the 'British Railways' sketch, where the Gang do a version of the banging door routine seen in *The Robert Dhéry* Show (22 February 1957). Best of all is Bud Flanagan standing at the footlights in his battered hat and joking with Ronnie Munro and the orchestra – you can almost feel a great wave of affection from the audience for this great trouper. One gets the impression of a master, holding the whole theatre in the palm of his hand, with the audience loving every minute. This is the closest that any item in the Hylton collection comes to achieving what Jack Hylton was probably setting out to do with his programmes.

The programme is also possibly the closest modern audiences are likely to get to seeing the genuine antics of the Crazy Gang, and as such it is one of the most outstanding items in the Hylton collection. It is certainly superior to *Friday Night with the Crazy Gang* (5 October 1956), in which the atmosphere of a live performance has been lost. One does wonder what the first of the Crazy Gang's programmes, transmitted live on 24 April 1956, was like. It went down well with critics, especially Bud Flanagan fan Peter Black, who asked for: 'more, please'. The Konyots were not in *Jokers Wild,* they were appearing in another Hylton show at the Adelphi.

JUMP FOR JOY
(TX 4.7.57)
'Jack Hylton and Chesney Allen Present *Jump For Joy* Extracts from the Summer Show South Parade Pier, Southsea. By Arrangement with David Evans.' *Jump For Joy* is a marvellous record of a traditional seaside summer show, with a mixture of comedy, music and dance. Reg Dixon and Sally Barnes each do individual turns as well as appearing together, and Dixon sings his self-penned theme tune, 'Confidentially'. Arnley and Gloria perform a comedy routine and the Three Skylarks sing and dance. The programme finishes with the whole cast singing 'I Do Like to Be Beside The Seaside'.

Credits
Those appearing were Reg Dixon, Sally Barnes, Arnley and Gloria, The Three Skylarks, Len & Les Rogers, Margaret Heath, Michael Ryan, Wendy Brandon, Len Astor.

Orchestra under the direction of Jack Frere; Designed by Roy Stannard; An Associated-Rediffusion Telerecording.

TV Times credits: Ernest Arnley and Gloria Day, Eleanor Beam's Eight Southsea Belles.

Staged by Stanley Willis-Croft; Directed by Peter Croft.

Notes
The Three Skylarks were Margaret Leggett, Joy Pollitt and Audrey Williams, three ex-Tiller girls. Reg Dixon is quoted in newspapers as saying he hoped

94

perhaps he had found a new partner, but he is obviously the star since he was paid £250 whereas Sally Barnes got £80.

The show was telerecorded on Friday 28 June 1957 beween 2.30 p.m. and 4 p.m. in Studio Two, Wembley. The company got the 7.27 a.m. train from Portsmouth and Southsea station which got to Waterloo at 9.14 a.m. A coach took them from Waterloo to Wembley, and the whole journey was reversed after the telerecording. The props and costumes had been brought up the night before and returned to Southsea on the Friday night. Presumably this meant that the Friday night show went ahead as usual. Rehearsals were on Saturday 22 June, Hippodrome Brighton, 10.30 a.m. to 5.40 p.m. and 27 June, Studio Two Wembley, 10 a.m. to 1 p.m.

LIVING IT UP
This series was intended to be a television version of the old BBC radio series *Band Waggon*.

LIVING IT UP (TX 10.5.57)
Arthur Askey and Richard Murdoch live in a flat atop A-R's Television House. Anthea Askey appears as herself, Danny Ross as a daffy props boy and Billy Percy is the milk and postman. At the end Askey says they have used these shows as a sort of trailer to see if he and Dickie would get on again after eighteen years; he says they hope to see the viewers again in the autumn.

Credits
Appearing with Arthur Askey were Richard Murdoch, Anthea Askey, Danny Ross, Billy Percy, Hugh Morton.

Script by Kavanagh Productions Ltd; Settings by Roy Stannard; Produced and directed by Eric Fawcett.

A Jack Hylton Production for Associated-Rediffusion.

Notes
This was live and telerecorded. The original idea was to do four shows, the fourth to have been filmed at the end of April for transmission on 26 May 1957. Arthur Askey got paid £750 per show. The series got a favourable reaction from the critics, although the second in the series was faded out before the end. Askey is reported as saying he wanted shows recorded so that they could be exported. He is also reported as saying that he prefers to do the shows live as they have no hope of selling telerecordings.

(TX 27.10.58)
Once again Murdoch and Askey are about to be thrown out of their flat by the Director General, so they have to resort to a spot of blackmail. After the credits Askey comes on camera again and says that programme two will be next week.

He makes comments about the audience not laughing and says that they are doing much better now that the programme is over.

Credits
Arthur Askey was *Living It Up* with Richard Murdoch and Danny Ross, Hugh Morton, Billy Percy, Leila Williams.

Billy Ternent and his Orchestra; Settings by Robert Freemantle; Script by Sid Colin and Talbot Rothwell; Directed by Bill Hitchcock.

A Jack Hylton Network Production for Associated-Rediffusion.

Notes
This show was 10th in the TAM Ratings. It had a rating of 67 and was viewed in 3,850,000 homes. In the following week's show Askey apparently kept making comments about the unfavourable critical reaction to the first show. Philip Purser wrote in the *News Chronicle* of 28 October 1958: 'Askey has such a boisterous genius for bursting through the fabric of any TV show that anything he does is watchable. But these two kindly, likeable and talented men deserve better material.'

Peter Black said in the *Daily Mail* of 28 October 1958: 'In its 27 minutes I counted two jokes that sounded as though someone was trying. The rest were typical of a lazy show that was being flung into the public's face like a gesture of complaint.'

Norman Cook wrote in the *Liverpool Echo* of 28 October 1958: 'Askey is television's throw-back to the circus clown or a provincial music-hall comic at his crudest and corniest ... But I cannot help hoping that the day will come when, thanks largely to television, our taste in comedy will have matured sufficiently for us to be less dependent on the capering clown and more attached to the subtle comedy actor ... Askey can still be very funny. But his style of comedy has outlived its age.'

LOVE AND KISSES
This was the stage sequel to the Arthur Askey play which had become the film *The Love Match*. *Love and Kisses* had been running at the Grand Theatre in Blackpool throughout the summer of 1955, and was one of the first programmes filmed for Jack Hylton Television Productions Ltd. It was shot by a company called Luckwin Productions. The film was initially split into five segments and transmitted by A-R on Fridays from 4 November to 2 December 1955, topped and tailed by live comments from Arthur Askey. The version related below is a complete film which was transmitted as such on ABC TV.

(TX 23.12.56 ON ABC)
Bill Brown, formerly an engine driver, is now landlord of a pub. We are gradually introduced to all the characters: Rose and Percy, Bill's children; Sal, their

mother; Emma, her friend; Alf a milkman and Rose's gormless boyfriend; Wally, Emma's even more gormless, stuttering husband, who is also Bill's friend and former colleague; Terence Steel, a producer and leading man, who is appearing at the newly re-opened theatre next door. After much comic business in the pub, much of which concerns poking fun at poor Alf, Bill and Wally eventually manage to get involved with the play that Terence is producing, and cause mayhem.

Credits
A comedy by Glynn [sic] Melvyn

Rose	Anthea Askey
Percy	Ian Gardiner
Sal	Lally Bowers
Emma	Barbara Miller
Alf	Danny Ross
Wally	Glenn Melvyn
Bill	Arthur Askey
Terence	Bernard Graham
Mr Seymour	Leonard Williams
Pam	Margaret Anderson
The Play	Directed by Richard Bird

Settings by John Russell; Television Direction Maclean Rogers; Transferred to the Screen by Bill Luckwell and D.E.A. Winn.

Produced by Jack Hylton.

Notes
This was initially shown over five nights on A-R. It had been split into five episodes and Arthur Askey appeared live on screens before and after each episode to introduce and explain the story, using flashbacks. Philip Purser said in the *Daily Mail* of 19 November 1955: 'The thinness of each instalment is padded out with introductory comments by Arthur Askey and the author Glenn Melvyn, which grow sillier every week.' A writer in *Commercial TV News* of 2 December 1955 pointed out: 'Even Arthur Askey seemed perturbed this week. After the flashback which, being out of context, made no sense at all — he told viewers: "I don't know why they chose to show you that bit." This week's episode was cut off almost in the middle of a sentence. Mr Askey looked a little upset as he exclaimed to viewers: "I don't know what happened there, they didn't even finish the scene."'

Love and Kisses was a sequel to *The Love Match*, also based on a play by Glenn Melvyn. Hylton obviously had thoughts of selling the production abroad, as the performers were contracted for World as well as UK and Commonwealth rights. The play was being performed by the company at the Grand Theatre, Blackpool, and the decision was taken to film it in London because that would be considerably cheaper than filming it at Blackpool — £6,425 as opposed to £8,000. As it was not adapted for television, four cameras and two sound units were placed in different parts of the Princes Theatre in London, and the cast performed the play before an invited audience. Arthur Askey had wanted to perform before an ordinary paying audience, but had to concede that because many of the seats would have their view obstructed by cameras, theatre-goers might object. Also, some seats would not be available for sale, so the Grand would be losing revenue.

Bernard Graham, who played Terence Steel, was born Bernard Popley. He later changed his name to Bernard Youens and achieved fame as Stan Ogden in *Coronation Street.*

MAKE ME LAUGH

A fiasco of a game show, imported from America, in which members of the public tried to stay straight-faced whilst the Crazy Gang attempted to make them laugh. For every second they held out the contestants would win five shillings. The first recording went so badly that the second was cancelled and other comedians were brought in to try and assist the Gang. It didn't work, and this series was one of Hylton's most abject failures, and the Crazy Gang's last TV appearance under his banner.

(TX 15.9.58)
Mr John Phillips of London, Bus Conductor, 1'39", £24 15/-
Barbara Castle, WRACTA, Medical Orderley, 18, breeds chickens, 2' 2", £30 10/-.
Tommy Yeardye of London, 3 mins, £90
Brian Reece (PC 49) appearing in *The Tunnel of Love* at Her Majesty's, 1' 41", £25 5/-.
Mrs Artois of London, 80, 1', £15. Chesney Allen gives her 5/- for every year of her age as well, so she gets £35 in all.
Leslie Watkins of London, TV Critic of the *Daily Sketch*, 2' 13", £33 5/-.

Watkins had bet that the Crazy Gang couldn't make him laugh, and they had to resort to covering him with flour and water until he smiled. He then offered to give the money to charity and suggested that he go to a London store, buy lots of toys and take them to a children's orphanage. He then asked the Crazy Gang to help him deliver them. He also asked the *Sketch*'s critic, Neville Randall, to give the show a dirty write-up. This sequence was obviously added later.

Credits
Hosted by Chesney Allen, Bud Flanagan, Nervo and Knox, Naughton and Gold, 'Monsewer' Eddie Grey. Announcer: Dick Norton, Escort: Sue Ruskin.

Televised by arrangement with Mort Green and George Foster; Settings by Robert Freemantle.

TV Times: Directed by Bill Hitchcock

A Jack Hylton Production for Associated-Rediffusion

Notes

Leslie Watkins issued his challenge in the *Daily Sketch* of 4 September 1958, when he said of the Crazy Gang: 'These are men who have brought laughter to millions. But they'll find this assignment too tough for them. I'm certain, for instance, that they couldn't make ME laugh to order.' The next day's editions covered the fact that Bud Flanagan had rung Watkins up and accepted his challenge. Watkins would be telerecording the programme that night at the Wembley Studios. Neville Randall did indeed give the show a dirty write-up. The toys went to the Maude Nathan orphanage at Crystal Palace. The *Jewish Chronicle* of 26 September 1958 reported the visit of Flanagan, Naughton, Gold and Watkins to the Maude Nathan Home for Little Children with the said toys.

A competition was held to find 'The girl with the happiest laugh' to introduce *Make Me Laugh*. Two hundred young women were interviewed, and ITV viewers voted eighteen-year-old, 37-24-38, Sue Ruskin their favourite.

Tommy Yeardye was a muscle-man and former escort of Diana Dors.

There was a lot of coverage in the papers about the size of the prizes being given away by ITV and this was considered money for old rope. Many people applied to be on it.

James Thomas wrote in the *Daily Express* of 16 September 1958: 'The Gang may as well stop trying to find the answer to TV. It will always elude them. Watered-down by telefilm, split up into a billion electronic particles, the old-timers lose their flesh and blood. The more I see of their TV disasters the more I beg Mr Hylton to leave them in the Victoria Palace.'

The programme ranked 8th in the ratings, watched in 4,085,000 homes.

(TX 22.9.58)
Edward Greenbury of London, Postman, 2'37", £39 5/-
Sergeant Major Brady of the Royal Hospital Chelsea, 3 mins, £90
Mary Lewis of Hampstead, Nurse, 18", £4 10/-
Evelyn Laye, 3 mins, £90
Mr and Mrs Reeve of Paddington, trolleybus driver and housewife, 1'40", £25.

Introduced by Sue Ruskin, then Chairman Chesney Allen. The Crazy Gang are ushered in by Eddie Gray and are joined by Arthur English and Davy Kaye. Chesney Allen follows exactly the same formula with every contestant, asking them what they do and whether they have any hobbies. He seems extremely ill at ease when not following a script.

The Chelsea Pensioner is full of quips and is actually funnier than the comedians trying to make him laugh. Mary Lewis brought a rowdy reaction from the men in the audience.

Credits

Chesney Allen tried to control Bud Flanagan, Nervo and Knox, Naughton and Gold, 'Monsewer' Eddie Gray, Arthur English, Davy Kaye. Directed by Douglas Hurn.

Davy Kaye is now appearing at the Embassy Club.

A Jack Hylton Network Production for Associated-Rediffusion.

Notes
Ranked 8th in the TAM ratings; watched in 3,801,000 homes.

(TX 29.9.58)
Mr Lewis of London, Milkman, 3 mins, £90
Mrs Elsie Hope of Manchester, 2'59", £44 15/-
Mr Leonard of Hackney, Hairdresser, 2'10", £32 10/-
Jack Solomons, 2'25", £36 5/-
Mr and Mrs Marriott from Manor Park, London, he works for a newspaper, she is a housewife, 2'14", £33 10/-
Mrs Kay Lawrence of London, rather posh English teacher, 1' 23", £21 15/-

This episode has no opening titles, and goes straight into the first contestant. It is also very poor quality; the original has obvously been damaged.

No closing credits but
Chesney Allen, Crazy Gang, Freddie Sales, Derek Roy, Davy Kaye, Al Burnett.

TAM rating of 64; viewed in 3,642,000 homes

(TX 6.10.58)
Mr Tony O'Brian from Tanganika, West Africa, Professional Hunter, 54", £13 10/-
Mrs Kathleen Saint of New Croft, Char Lady, 1'53", £28 5/-
Mr Paul Witherford-Young of London, General Secretary of the London Federation of Boys' Clubs, 3 mins, £90
Harry Weetman, golfer, 3 mins, £90
Mr Burling of East Ham, Taxi Driver, 3 mins, £90
Miss Sheila Wingrow of Catford, 20, secretary, models in her spare time, 2' 23", £35 15/-. (This contestant inspired lots of jokes about Tommy Steele, and lots of wolf whistles from the audience.)

No credits, but
Chesney Allen, Crazy Gang, Eddie Gray, Freddie Sales, Derek Roy, Davy Kaye, Arthur English, Al Burnett, Sue Ruskin.

TV Times credits
Director Douglas Hurn

Notes
The *Daily Mirror* of 6 October 1958 said that the reinforcements were recruited because the Crazy Gang could only look in for a short while as they were filming at Shepperton for *Clowns in Clover*. (This is possibly *Life is a Circus*).

100

In *TV Mirror* of 11 October 1958 Shirley Long wrote in his *Look Out* column: 'Jack Hylton fears that he will never smile again ... To the people in the studio working on the show the terrifying thing was the thoroughness with which contestants entered into the idea. They did not crack their faces at anything or anybody from the moment they walked in. ... It was Jack Hylton, sitting in the control room of the studio, hardly able to bring himself to watch the slaughter of the comedians, who noted that while so many contestants could remain frozen faced with the studio audience falling about in gales of laughter, it was usually some quite small gag or joke, greeted by silence in the studio, which finally made them laugh.'

TAM Rating of 64; viewed in 3,648,000 homes

(TX 13.10.58)
Sue Ruskin doesn't introduce Chesney Allen, the announcer does.
Mrs Irene Oliver of Kennington, Housewife, 2'31", £37 15/-
Mr Martin of Thornton Heath, Butcher, 1'23", £20 15/-
Margaret and Josephine Collins, 18 year-old twins, hope to be singers, 3 mins, £90 each.
Lady Docker, 2' 31", £37 15/-. (She knows that she is likely to laugh at Al Burnett, and indeed does so. She wants the money to go to her favourite charity, though it is never stated which one.)
Mr Thomas Stephen, Purley, Accountant, 2'39", £39 15/-
Miss Helen Arkinson, Scotland, 1'25", £21 5/-

Credits
Bud Flanagan, Nervo & Knox, Naughton and Gold, 'Monsewer' Eddie Gray, Al Burnett, Derek Roy, Davy Kaye, Freddie Sales, Chairman Chesney Allen, Announcer Dick Norton, Escort Sue Ruskin. Directed by Douglas Hurn.

Davy Kaye is now appearing at the Embassy Club.

Notes
TAM rating of 57; viewed in 3,259,000 homes.

(TX 20.10.58)
Mr John Atkins of London, makes handmade shoes, 1'23", £20 15/-
Mr Harry Meadows of London, Nightclub Manager, 1' 39", £24.15/-
Miss Ada Hartley of Redcar, Yorks, 84, 2'29", £37 5/-
Mr Eric Parsons, London, Insurance Broker, 3 mins, £90
Jimmy Hill of Fulham FC, 1' 47", £26 15/-
Miss Barbara Webb, Jersey, Radiographer, 14", £3 10/-
William Hammett of Marylebone, Ambulance Driver, 1' 21", £20 5/-

Credits
Bud Flanagan, Nervo & Knox, Naughton and Gold, 'Monsewer' Eddie Gray, Al Burnett, Derek Roy, Davy Kaye, Freddie Sales, Chairman Chesney Allen, Announcer Dick Norton, Escort Sue Ruskin. Directed by Douglas Hurn.

Davy Kaye is now appearing at the Embassy Club.

MUSIC BOX

This was a series of variety shows, with a different host and guest artists each week.

(TX 4.1.57)
The opening dance routine with George Tapps and his dancers seems to go on forever. Tommy Trinder hosts the show and also appears as Harry Champion singing 'Any Old Iron' and in drag singing 'Strolling Down the Strand with a Banana in My Hand'. Comedy is provided by Desmond Walter-Ellis and Patachou sings 'I Love Paris', 'C'est si Bon', 'Autumn Leaves', 'Pigalle', 'Sous les ponts de Paris', 'La vie en rose'.

Credits
Patachou (now appearing at the Adelphi Theatre London), George Tapps and his dancers (now appearing at the Adelphi Theatre London), Desmond Walter-Ellis, Derek Tansley, Michael Hogan, and Tommy Trinder (now appearing at the Adelphi Theatre London), Jean Wynser (now appearing at the Victoria Palace London) and the Adelphi Boys and Girls.

Choreography by George Tapps; Sketch written by Godfrey Harrison and Desmond Walter-Ellis; Billy Ternent and his Orchestra; Directed by Kenneth Carter.

Notes
This show is absolutely shameless. It is one enormous plug for Jack Hylton's theatre shows.

(TX 18.1.57)
Bud Flangan hosts. Ivy Benson and her Girls' Band play 'Lady Be Good', 'Halleluia' and 'See You Later, Alligator', with Gloria Russell as vocalist. 'Monsewer' Eddie Gray performs a comedy juggling act. His partner is possibly Danny Gray. Jean Wynser sings 'Take More Exercise' while the Tiller Girls dance. Flanagan sings 'Dreaming', 'Leave Me Alone, Let Me Wander' and 'Life is What You Make it', and is joined by female singers and the Radio Revellers.

Credits
In The Music Box were Bud Flanagan, 'Monsewer' Eddie Gray, The Radio Revellers, Jean Wynser and the John Tiller Girls, who are all now appearing in *These Foolish Kings* at the Victoria Palace London, Ivy Benson and her Girls' Band.

Settings by Kenneth Carey; Directed by Kenneth Carter.

TV Times credits
Director Douglas Hurn; Musical direction by Billy Ternent; Settings by John Clements.

(TX 1.2.57)
This show has no main host, but contains a mixture of variety turns, including a singer, a comedy whistling act and Rosalina Neri. The second half of the programme consists of the Crazy Gang performing a sketch from their show *These Foolish Kings*. It is an excerpt from *A Midsummer Night's Dream* with Bud Flanagan (Pyramus), 'Monsewer' Eddie Gray (Wall), Charlie Naughton (Thisbe), Teddy Knox (Peter Quince), Jimmy Gold (Moonshine), Jimmy Nervo (Lion).

Credits
The Crazy Gang (who are now appearing in *These Foolish Kings* at the Victoria Palace), Rosalina Neri, Les Joyeux Rossignols, Bryan Johnson with the Malcolm Clare Group.

Billy Ternent and his Orchestra; Settings by Kenneth Carey; Director Douglas Hurn.

Notes
Les Rossignols (nightingales) had favoured wearing tartan ever since their first appearance in a Paris nightclub where their kilts were: 'amusingly different' (*Birmingham Mail*, 27 January 1958)

(TX 8.2.57)
Terry-Thomas is the host. Ivy Benson and her band play 'Lover', 'Rock a Beatin' Boogie' and 'The Birth of the Blues'. Rosalina Neri does three numbers and Luigi Infantina sings two. Terry-Thomas appears in a rather awkward sketch with Leslie Mitchell, tells some jokes and sings a song.

Credits
Terry-Thomas introduced Luigi Infantino, Rosalina Neri, Leslie Mitchell, Ivy Benson and her Orchestra. Settings by Roy Stannard; Directed by Eric Fawcett

TV Times credits: Designed by Frank Gilman.

Notes
Recorded at Studio One Wembley, Friday 1 February 1957. Terry-Thomas's script was written by Dennis Castle.

(TX 15.2.57)
No sound for first part of programme. It is hosted by Leslie Sarony who introduces a young girl he says will go far: None other than Tommy Trinder in drag singing 'Strolling Down the Strand', as seen on *Music Box* (4 January 1957). Leslie Sarony also sings the song, which he says he wrote for Trinder, along with the next song, 'I Like Riding on a Choo Choo Choo'. Michael and Shirley Davis perform a dance routine. Max Miller sings 'A Pocketful of Sunshine' and then 'I've Got a Pocketful of Blue Jokes'. He then tells a

couple of jokes and finishes with another song, 'Isn't it Grand to See Someone Smile'.

Credits
Leslie Sarony introduced Max Miller, Michael and Shirley Davis (currently appearing at the Embassy Club), Shirley Ryan and Tommy Trinder.
Billy Ternent and his Orchestra; Settings by Frank Gillman; Directed by Eric Fawcett.

(TX 1.3.57)
Australian comedian Terry Scanlon is this week's host. There is comedy sketch from Lauri Lupino Lane and George Truzzi, who perform a slapstick Robin Hood sketch. The Tiller girls do a ballet routine and Australian singer Maggie Fitzgibbon sings 'Can I Steal a Little Love' and 'Got the World on a String', accompanied by Billy Ternent and the orchestra. Terry Scanlon then tells a few more jokes, including one about marijuana, and introduces the final guest, George Raft. He does a dance which he says he introduced to Britain in 1926, accompanied by Jack Hylton's orchestra. He dances to 'Top Hat, White Tie and Tails' and 'Sweet Georgia Brown', accompanied by the Tiller Girls.

Credits
Terry Scanlon Introduced George Raft, Maggie Fitgibbon, Lauri Lupino Lane and George Truzzi, The John Tiller Girls. Routine by Barbara Aitken.

Billy Ternent and his Orchestra; Settings by Frank Gillman; Directed by Eric Fawcett.

Notes
George Raft was sixty-one at the time. He had been in the UK with a view to making a film, but had pulled out as he was dissatisfied with the script. He appeared in *Music Box* as a last minute replacement for George Formby, who was unable to appear owing to laryngitis. Recorded at Studio One, Wembley, Friday 22 February 1957.

THE ROBERT DHÉRY SHOW
Hylton had brought Dhéry and his company to London from Paris, and they had been a great success. Robert Dhéry himself has a certain charm, and some of the sketches are very funny, mainly due to the skill of his troupe and their excellent comic timing. The style of comedy seems to have been rather different for the time and the repeated use of certain 'characters' like the man with the exploding electric guitar or the man who growls like a dog (Jacques Legras) builds up the comedy. On stage it would perhaps have made more sense, but it would still be entertaining if the viewer had watched all the programmes and recognised the various characters. The programmes were recorded at Studio One, Wembley.

PARIS MUSIC HALL

(TX 22.2.57)
Includes a comic ballet sequence and the shower cubicle routine. Part Two has no sound.

Credits
Robert Dhéry introduced Colette Brosset, Pierre Olaf, Phillipe Dumat, Roger Caccia, Jacques Legras, Ross Parker, Henri Pennec, Laurence Soupault, The Garrick Rockettes, Pamela Austin, Peter Bentley, Maureen Hill, Michael Austin-Kent.

Orchestra conducted by Robert Probst; Production Manager for Jack Hylton John Russell; Produced and Directed by Robert Dhéry and Eric Fawcett; Robert Dhéry and his company are appearing in *La Plume de ma Tante* at the Garrick Theatre, London.

A Jack Hylton Production for Associated-Rediffusion

Notes
Real names were Robert and Marie-Claudette Fourrey. Robert Dhéry was thirty-five, Colette Brosset (his wife) thirty-three. They had been appearing at the Garrick for fifteen months. The show was very popular and had even been seen by members of the Royal Family — the Queen, Duke of Edinburgh, Princess Margaret and Queen Mother. According to the *Daily Mirror* of 22 February 1957, Hylton: 'banned two of the sauciest scenes' from being transferred to TV. They were a sketch in which two men get trapped in a French urinal,and a typical French bedroom sketch. Philip Purser remembers that on stage there was quite a bit of nudity, for example in the shower sketch everyone in the showers was nude, and a lot of bare bottoms were seen.
   In a memo to Bryan Michie and Hugh Charles, Hylton said: 'If Robert Dhéry is doing the script himself for this series we will have to pay him £100 per script for material which I do not already own'. Hylton had bought the rights to a lot of Dhéry's sketches for use by the Crazy Gang.

PARIS MUSIC HALL

(TX 8.3.57)
Sketches include 'La Corrida', 'Adam and Eve' and the famous 'Frere Jacques' bell-ringing monks (also used by the Crazy Gang in their revue *Jokers Wild*).

Credits
As before, plus Caid the horse.

Notes
M Bernard Vanot got paid £20 for the appearance of his horse, Caid.

HIGH SOCIETY
(TX 22.3.57)
Includes a ballroom scene, adapted as 'Tedwardian Nights' for the Crazy Gang revue *Jokers Wild*, and the 'Song of the Balloon'. Also 'Mannequins of Paris' and a very funny 'French Chamber Music' sketch.

Credits
As before.

TV Times credit: Choreography by Colette Brosset

LE FINAL DE PARIS
(TX 29.3.57)
Sketches include one about the French bicycle police, the 'Song of the Cat', 'Dream Rendezvous' and 'Queen of the Striptease'. At the end Dhéry says goodbye to viewers and says they are going back to Paris.

Credits
As before

(TX 19.5.58)
The second of two shows based on Dhéry's observations of English life, the first having gone out live. Sketches include one about trying to make a Guardsman laugh, one on paperwork, and a rather sweet little one about an oyster opener. Finishes with the whole cast doing a marching routine dressed as Guardsmen.

Credits
Appearing with Robert Dhéry were Colette Brosset and Pierre Olaf, Roger Caccia, Jacques Legras, Phillipe Dumat, Ross Parker, Henri Parker, Simone Duhart, Yvette Dolvia, Robert Rollis, Laurence Soupault, Grosso and Modo, Yvonne Constant, Manuela, Elizabeth Fanty, Annie Gardel, Brigitte Uzal, Ariel Domerg, Daniele Roma, Francoise Dally, Michael Kent, Desmond Ainsworth.

Script by Robert Dhéry; Original Music and arrangements by Gerard Calvi; Choreography by Colette Brosset; Musical Director Billy Ternent; English lyrics by Ross Parker; Directed for Television by Bill Hitchcock.

Notes
This is not based on a UK stage show, but on the show Dhéry did in Paris after returning from London, *Les pommes a l'Anglaise*. He came over to get a bit of peace and quiet to write a film script and at the same time did a forty-five-minute live programme, and then immediately telerecorded this programme for showing two weeks later. He had broken a rib and was consequently working with a chest bound in plaster of paris. Achieved a TAM rating of 35; watched in 1,958,000 homes.

106

THE ROSALINA NERI SHOW

After having appeared in numerous Jack Hylton programmes since early 1956, Rosalina Neri finally got her own show, with co-host Ivor Emmanuel, in 1959. There were two series of *The Rosalina Neri Show* in 1959, and both were a mixture of solo spots and duets for Rosalina and Ivor, plus dance routines with other young singers and dancers. The programmes were livened up by Rosalina sometimes forgetting her words, getting her scarf caught, or Emmanuel bumping into scenery. Some programmes also have guest artists.

After her relationship with Hylton ended, Rosalina returned to Italy and was last heard of in the mid-60s, singing opera under her mother's maiden name, Angela Baldi.

(TX 26.3.59)
Songs from Rosalina include 'I Don't Know Why', 'You Made Me Love You', 'Lili Marlene', while Ivor sings 'Danny Boy' and 'Luck Be a Lady'. Both sing a selection of tunes from 'The Merry Widow' and end with Rosalina's theme song, *'Souvenir D'Italie'*. Thorn Kelling plays guitar and sings.

Credits
Rosalina Neri, Ivor Emmanuel, Thorn Kelling.

Arrangements by Musical Director Billy Ternent; Choreography by Gilbert Vernon; Settings by Denis Wreford; Directed by Mark Lawton.

Notes
The 'appearance' by Thorn Kelling seems to be film of him which was shot for one of Hylton's first programmes in 1955.

(TX 2.4.59)
Rosa's songs include *'Je Veux'* and 'When You Hold My Hand/Paradise', 'Oh Ho, Ha Ha', 'Baby Doll', *'Arrivederci Roma'* and some unrecognisable Italian and French ones. Ivor sings 'Long Before I Met You', 'Sit Down You're Rocking the Boat' and *'Finiculli Funiculla'*. They duet on *'Poppa Piccolino'*. Sibley and Usher perform some ballet.

Credits
As above.

Guest Artists Antoinette Sibley and Graham Usher (Appear with kind permission of the General Administrator Covent Garden)

(TX 18.9.59)
Rosalina sings 'Diamonds Are a Girl's Best Friend', 'Nothing Could Be Finer Than To Be in Carolina' and an Italian song apparently called 'Wait For Me'. Ivor sings 'Softly' and 'You Gotta Have Heart'. Stephane Grappelly plays two numbers, including 'Lady Be Good'. Rosalina and Ivor, in a schoolroom scene, sing 'That Was a Cute Little Rhyme' and 'An Apple for the Teacher' and end with *'Souvenir d'Italie'*.

Credits
As above.

Guest Artist Stephane Grappelli.

TV Times credits: Pamela Barrie, Dennis Egan, Virginia Mason, Gerald Mordon, Joyce Queale.

Notes
Some papers reported in January 1964 that Rosalina had been burgled in Milan losing fur coats and jewellery worth £46,000, so she obviously knew diamonds really were a girl's best friend.

(TX 25.9.59)
Rosalina sings a new Italian song (title unknown), 'I Wanna Get Married', 'Waiting at the Church', 'Now I Have to Call Him Father', 'It Had To Be You', 'Autumn Leaves' and *'Pigalle'*. Ivor sings 'Love, Wonderful Love', *Luna rossa'*, 'Bridges of Paris' and 'Valentina' and then he and Rosa sing *'C'est si bon'*, *'Oh la la oui oui'* and *'Souvenir d'Italie'*.

Credits
As above.

Notes
According to the *Star* of 25 September 1959, Rosalina was in Milan auditioning for a musical comedy at the time this programme was transmitted.

(TX 2.10.59)
Rosalina sings 'You Do Something to Me', 'I'm in The Mood for Love', *'Sarracino'*, *'Na Voche'*, 'You'll Never Know', 'Falling in Love Again' and *'Souvenir d'Italie'*. Ivor sings *'Seronate'*, 'Lullaby of Broadway', 'Wagon Train', 'Don't Fence Me in', 'I'm an Old Cowhand and 'Louisianna Hayride'. Osian Ellis plays the harp.

Credits
As above.

Guest Artist Osian Ellis

(TX 9.10.59)
Rosalina sings something in Italian, possibly *'Luna'*, *'La vie en rose'*, *'Ciao, ciao, bambino'*, 'Give My Regards To Broadway', 'Oh, Oh, Antonio', 'Every Little While', 'Don't Forget' and *'Souvenir d'Italie'*. Ivor sings 'Ramona', 'Waiting for the Robert E. Lee', 'On the Banks of the Wabash', 'By the Light of the Silvery Moon' and 'Lady of Spain'.

Credits
As above.

This is virtually the same routine Rosalina did in *Jack Hylton's Monday Show* (10 February 1958).

(TX 16.10.59)
Rosalina talks! She introduces a new Italian song called '*Pasqualino*'. She then says that she has had many letters asking her to sing '*Quaglioni*', which she proceeds to do. She also sings 'Ma, He's Making Eyes at Me', 'You'd Be Surprised', 'If You Could Care for Me', 'Am I Wasting My Time on You', 'Oh Ho, Ha Ha' and '*Souvenir d'Italie*'. Ivor sings 'So In Love', 'Rosanna', 'The Continental' and a song which sounds as if it's called 'Walking Along, Kaplang Kaplong'. Together they sing 'Boom'.

Credits
As above.

Musical Director Billy Miller; Arrangements by Billy Ternent.

(TX 23.10.59)
Rosalina sings 'Undecided', '*Oui, oui, oui*', 'September in the Rain', 'You Go To My Head' and '*Volare*'. Ivor sings 'This Nearly Was Mine', 'Donkey Serenade' and '*O sole mio*' in English. Rosalina ends by singing '*Souvenir d'Italie*' as the credits roll, and they all drink glasses of wine. Rosa and Ivor are joined by Billy Ternent, who comes on and has a glass of Chianti with them and joins in the singing. Rosa looks as if she has been knocking back something a little bit stronger during most of this part.

Credits
As before.

Notes
Peter Forster wrote in the *Spectator* of 30 October 1959: 'Not the least memorable moment last week came in one of Jack Hylton's new Rosalina Neri half-hours (A-R). Our blonde, Italian wimple-with-a-dimple, was singing of autumn leaves in front of an outsize wooden frame shaped in the letters RN, from which autumn leaves duly fluttered down. Miss Neri is never a girl to hide her assets, and lo, a leaf hovered and hesitated and then alighted upon the convenient ledge of her corsage; but Miss Neri sang on. A moment later, possibly because the leaf weighed as much as the last straw, her shoulder-strap slipped down: Miss Neri sang on, and her expression changed no more than in any of her previous songs. Such nonchalance can rarely be seen on television, and it only goes to show that if you give somebody a series often enough something entertaining may eventually happen.'

The TV Critic in the *Times Educational Supplement* of 27 November 1959 said: 'She is above all a past mistresss in the gentle art of upstaging, with a talent rising at times to genius for forgetting the words at the precise moment when it will have the most devastating effect on the rest of the cast.'

SOMETHING IN THE CITY

This series was based on sketches from a Sid Caesar show called *Caesar's Hour*. 'The Commuters' had been one of the most popular recurring sketches in *Caesar's Hour*. As Hylton and A-R owned the rights to many of the scripts, 'The Commmuters' ones were used as the basis for *Something in the City*. Artists originally considered for parts of the suburb-dwellers included Daniel Massey, Bernard Cribbins, Gerald Harper, Eric Thompson, Michael Bryant, Des O'Connor, Henry MacGee, Millicent Martin and Barbara Windsor. The series concerns the lives of three couples, where the husbands are 'something in the city' and the wives stay at home. However, the characters are caricatures, the situations trite and simplistic. The original scripts were probably anglicised by Eric Barker.

(TX 6.7.59)
This episode follows what happens when George is persuaded to buy Freddie's car, which turns out to be an old wreck.

Opening Credits
Peter Hammond and Diane Hart as Joe and Maisie Miller; Deryck Guyler and Pearl Hackney as Freddie and Phyl Chiddock; Eric Barker and Joan Benham as George and Betty Keyes.

Closing Credits
Music written and conducted by Basil Tait; Settings by Denis Wreford; Directed by Kenneth Carter.

A Jack Hylton Network Production for Associated-Rediffusion

Notes
It was Barker's first regular TV series for four years. The programme was recorded with a very small audience, in order to give the actors an indication of laughs and reactions, but was transmitted with an added laughter track. The option of videotaping was given by A-R, but was turned down as the addition of a laughter track would not have been possible.

(TX 13.7.59)
Betty Keyes becomes convinced that George is having an affair.

Credits
As above plus Leila Blake as Mrs Swak and Monica Moore as Miss Chandler and Mickey the Budgie, Caesar the Dog.

Notes
Much funnier than this plot is the moment when Freddie Chiddock's new secretary tells him: 'I do hope I shall satisfy you', and not a ribald chuckle is heard.

Peter Black wrote in the *Daily Mail* of 14 July 1959 that this episide: 'Staggered from cliché to cliché with an indifference to quality for which I can only hope that Barker is ashamed. It is very sad to watch an artist lowering his standards in this way'.

(TX 20.7.59)
The wives have decided that they are fed-up with housework, so Betty hires a pretty young French girl called Marie-Christine, much to the delight of all the men.

Credits
As before plus Marcelle Georgius as Marie-Christine, Michael Bird as Felix, Ralph Tovey as Landlord.

(TX 27.7.59)
In the first part of this episode, George is convinced that he is at death's door. In the second part, George's new moustache is a great favourite with all the ladies.

Credits
As before, plus Tom Chatto as Doctor Raley, with Vikki Hammond, Monica Moore, Rita Royce, Lesley Allen, Deirdre Benner, Ginette Edwards.

(TX 3.8.59)
The three couples decide to give up TV for a month.

Credits
As above, plus Monica Moore as Miss Chandler, with Barbara Adams, Arnold Locke, Humphrey Heathcote, Henry Drew, Colin Cunningham.

TOGETHER AGAIN
Flanagan and Allen are reunited for a nostalgic stroll through some of their most familiar songs and comic sketches.

(TX 5.4.57)
Sketches include a Tax Office one, and songs are 'Sending Out an S.O.S. for You', 'Home Town', 'Umbrella Man' and '*Au Revoir*'.

Credits
With Bud Flanagan and Chesney Allen, Max Bacon, George Stone, Dick James, Courtney Bromet, Raymond Graham, Jack Hylton's Young Ladies.

Billy Ternent and his Orchestra; Choreography Joan Davis; Script by Bud Flanagan; Settings by Kenneth Carey; Directed by John Phillips.

A Jack Hylton for Associated-Rediffusion Telerecording.

Notes

This was billed as Flanagan and Allen's first fully-fledged public show together since their break-up in 1946. The *Daily Herald* of 6 April 1957 reported: 'It is difficult to know whether this, one of the most famous partnerships in the business, has any attraction for today's youth. They may only see two old men indulging in cross-talk and broad humour and singing old songs like "Hometown" and "Umbrella Man".' The *Daily Telegraph* of 6 April 1957 said: 'Their act might have been preserved in a deep freeze under the Thames.'

The show was recorded (at the Wembley Studios) owing to Allen's ill health and the fact that Flanagan was appearing twice nightly with the Crazy Gang in *These Foolish Kings* at the Victoria Palace. They got £100 each per show.

(TX 19.4.57)
Sketches include one with Ches and Bud as a turf advisor and punter. Songs are 'Hey, Neighbour', 'Underneath The Arches', 'Down Every Street', 'Run Rabbit Run', '*Au Revoir*'.

Credits
With Bud Flanagan and Chesney Allen were the Radio Revellers, Peter Glaze, the George Mitchell Singers, Jack Hylton's Young Ladies.

Choreography Joan Davis; with Billy Ternent and his Orchestra; Script by Bud Flanagan; Settings by Kenneth Carey; Directed by John Phillips.

(TX 3.5.57)
Songs include 'Free', 'We'll Smile Again', 'Where the Arches Used to Be' and '*Au Revoir*'.

Credits
With Bud Flanagan and Chesney Allen were The Radio Revellers, Peter Glaze, Jane Hilary, George Stone, the Jack Hylton Dancers, the George Mitchell Singers.

Choreography Joan Davis; with Billy Ternent and his Orchestra; Script by Bud Flanagan; Settings by Kenneth Carey; Directed by John Phillips.

(TX 17.5.57)
Sketches include one about Ye Olde ITV, and one set in a restaurant. Songs are 'A Million Tears', 'Don't Believe Everything You Dream', 'Round the Back of the Arches' and '*Au Revoir*'.

Credits
With Bud Flanagan and Chesney Allen were the Radio Revellers, Peter Glaze, Jean Wynser, George Stone, Redvers Kyle, the Jack Hylton Dancers.

Dances arranged by Joan Davis; with Jack Ansell and his orchestra; Script by Bud Flanagan; Settings by Roy Stannard; Directed by John Phillips.

Notes
Bernard Levin wrote in the *Manchester Guardian* of 25 May 1957: 'I cannot but point out that *Together Again* strikes me as being in part pitiful and in part disgusting. Also — and this is the point — in part a wonderful feast of nostalgia and sentiment. This is the part in which Flanagan and Allen are neither joking nor acting, but singing songs. ... for a moment the screen radiates delight.'

(TX 31.5.57)
Sketches include 'Antimacassars and Old Lace' and songs are 'How Do You Do, Mr Right', 'Miss You', 'Maybe it's Because I'm a Londoner' and '*Au Revoir*'.

Credits
With Bud Flanagan and Chesney Allen were 'Monsewer' Eddie Grey, the Radio Revellers, Peter Glaze, George Stone, Maggie Fitzgibbon (now in caberet at Winston's Club), the Jack Hylton Dancers.

Dances arranged by Joan Davis; with Jack Ansell and his orchestra; Script by Bud Flanagan; Settings by Roy Stannard; Directed by John Phillips.

(TX 14.6.57)
Sketches include one about the French Foreign Legion and the Jockey sketch. Songs are 'What More Can I Say', 'Wanderers', 'Dreaming', 'I'll Get By' and '*Au Revoir*'.

Credits
With Bud Flanagan and Chesney Allen were The Radio Revellers, Peter Glaze, Lillemor Knudsen, George Stone, Lionel Gamlin, the Jack Hylton Dancers.

Dances arranged by Joan Davis; with Jack Ansell and his Orchestra; Script by Bud Flanagan; Settings by Roy Stannard; Directed by John Phillips.

Notes
The dance routine in this episode is hysterically funny. It is set around a swimming pool, and the floor is obviously so slippery that the bare-footed girls slide all over the place. One poor girl actually falls over — twice! George Stone, reported in Peter Black's *Daily Mail* 'Teleview' of 14 June 1957, says that each show took three or four days' rehearsal, whilst Flanagan was still doing twelve shows a week at the Victoria Palace.

THE TONY HANCOCK SHOW
This series was Hancock's first on television, and took a different format to his famous BBC TV one. Hancock and company appeared in a series of sketches, sometime linked, sometimes not, and because the programmes were performed live the various costume and scene changes were covered up by a song from June Whitfield or a dance sequence. It was not a particularly successful series, and the format changed for Hancock's second outing for Jack Hylton.

(TX 27.4.56)
Sketches include one set in a coffee bar and 'Come Back Little Streetcar'. Hancock and Whitfield also perform a flamenco dance routine. At one point in the programme Hancock says: 'I hope it isn't as bad as this at the BBC'.

Credits
Tony Hancock, June Whitfield, Dick Emery, Clive Dunn, John Vere, Pamela Deeming, The Guitarist - Eile Bibobi, The Teenagers.

Musical Numbers staged by Deirdre Vivian; Original Music and Lyrics by Christopher Hodder Williams; Musical Direction by Cyril Ornadel; Script by Eric Sykes and Larry Stephens; Settings by Henry Federer; Directed by Kenneth Carter.

A Jack Hylton Production for Associated-Rediffusion

Notes
Peter Black wrote in the *Daily Mail* of 28 April 1956: 'Tony Hancock, one of radio's funniest men, crossed over to TV last night for the first time in five years. The combination of Whitfield and Hancock, plus a script by Eric Sykes, ought to guarantee success, but the urbane satire of *Idiot Weekly* has temporarily spoiled us for the more knockabout comedy.'
Larry Stephens was to write some of *The Goon Show* scripts with Spike Milligan

(TX 4.5.56)
Sketches include one set in a library, with Hancock getting fed-up with having to get books off the top shelf all the time, and he and Whitfield do a spoof on Armand and Michaela Denis. Hancock does an exotic dance routine as Ram Hancock.

Credits
Tony Hancock, June Whitfield, Dick Emery, Clive Dunn, John Vere, Bernard Livesy, Jimmy White, Roy Bartley, The Teenagers.

Musical numbers staged by Deirdre Vivian; Original music and lyrics by Christopher Hodder Williams; Musical Direction by Cyril Ornadel; Script by Eric Sykes and Larry Stephens; Settings by Henry Federer; Directed by Kenneth Carter.

(TX 11.5.56)
This episode is less sketch based and follows a complete storyline in which Hancock is producing his seventh long-running musical in the last four weeks. This one is called 'Love Is Good'.

Credits
Tony Hancock, June Whitfield, Clive Dunn, John Vere, The Teenagers.

Musical Numbers Staged by Deirdre Vivian; The Barney Gilbraith Singers; Original Lyrics and Music by Christopher Hodder Williams; with Additional music by Kenny Powell; Musical Direction by Cyril Ornadel; Script by Eric Sykes; Directed by Kenneth Carter.

A Jack Hylton Production for Associated-Rediffusion

(TX 18.5.56)
The first sketch is a look at what would happen if court procedings were televised, the second concerns Chez Hancock, London's Britest Niterie, in which Hancock plays cloakroom attendant, waiter, chef, gypsy violinist and apache dancer.

Credits
Tony Hancock, June Whitfield, Clive Dunn, John Vere, Ronan O'Casey, Valerie Frazer, Cyril Renison, Lizabeth Cassay, The Teenagers.

Musical numbers staged by Deirdre Vivian; Original Lyrics and Music by Christopher Hodder Williams; Additional Music by Kenny Powell and Basil Tait; Musical Direction by Cyril Ornadel; Script by Eric Sykes; Settings by Henry Federer; Directed by Kenneth Carter;

Notes
Uncredited appearance by Eric Sykes in the courtroom sketch.

(TX 25.5.56)
Sketches include one with Hancock pretending to conduct the *Last Night of the Proms*, and a spoof on *Gun Law*. Throughout it all, Hancock is concerned that other members of the cast keep ruining things and decides to jump into the Thames.

Credits
Tony Hancock, June Whitfield, Robert Arden, Sam Kydd, Clive Dunn, John Vere, Dorothy Blythe, Neale Warrington, The Teenagers.

Musical Numbers staged by Deirdre Vivian; Original lyrics and Music by Christopher Hodder Williams, with Additional Music by Basil Tait and Kenny Powell; Musical Direction by Cyril Ornadel; Script by Eric Sykes; Directed by Kenneth Carter.

(TX 1.6.56)
Hancock auctions the remnants of the programme as it is the last of the series. For the rest of the episode the French detective Hercules Parrot attempts to solve a murder.

Credits
Tony Hancock, Hattie Jacques, Clive Dunn, John Vere, Ray Browne, Neale Warrington, The Teenagers and Valentine Dyall.

Original lyric and music by Christopher Hodder Williams; Musical Direction by Cyril Ornadel; Script by Eric Sykes; Settings by Henry Federer; Directed by Kenneth Carter.

Notes
June Whitfield was on a belated honeymoon, hence the appearance of Hattie Jacques in her stead.